A GREAT PARTY

DESIGNING THE PERFECT CELEBRATION

Rizzoli
NEW YORK

New York Paris London Milan

A GREAT PARTY

DESIGNING THE PERFECT CELEBRATION

Bryan Rafanelli

FOREWORD BY CHELSEA CLINTON

FOR MY MOTHER, CAROL ANN RAFANELLI,
THE PERSON WHO CELEBRATES EVERYTHING.

CONTENTS

FOREWORD
BY CHELSEA CLINTON

Bryan Rafanelli is a master storyteller and community builder. He is also generous-hearted and obsessed with details large and small. It is the magical combination of those traits that gives him the ability to highlight and support the important work of an organization, the culture and history of our country, and the love between two people. I have been fortunate enough to be part of Bryan's events as a speaker, an attendee, and a bride, and every event I've been to has felt unique and purposed for that cause and that moment. Nothing has ever felt superfluous. Nothing has ever felt repeated; it would never occur to Bryan to copy himself. The underlying reason for an event, be it an organization, a marriage, or a life, and the community gathered to celebrate it, has always been central to Bryan's planning, and his imagination and heart have been evident in every detail.

When we were planning our wedding, it was important to Marc and to me that my mother and grandmother be included at every step. Bryan understood this and took particular care to ensure that every meeting was accessible to my grandmother without her ever feeling like special care had been taken. He knew she would have been mortified to know we had planned font size and routes to look at venues around what would work for her. He also knew we wouldn't have it any other way. Bryan gave special attention to my grandmother's feedback on proposed color schemes, flowers, and food options. He also knew—as Marc and I did—that she had exquisite taste and was full of creativity, fun, and elegance. When we were at our wedding reception, I could see my grandmother's influence everywhere, as well as the love that we had shared my whole life, of which Marc was now and forever would be an important part.

I will always be most thankful to Bryan for the moments of seeing my grandmother's influence and love throughout our wedding planning and celebration. For the memories of laughing with her over menu selections and the varied shapes of succulents. Most of all, I will always treasure the joy Marc and I saw on her face every time we looked at her throughout our wedding celebration.

An event planned by Bryan that I was particularly proud to be a part of was the Big Sister Association of Greater Boston's sixtieth anniversary. For decades, Big Sister has worked to create and foster meaningful mentor relationships for girls to help them become the confident, competent, caring adults that every child deserves the chance to grow up and be. While the mayor of Boston and I both spoke, Bryan made sure that the girls and their mentors, past and present, were the center of the evening and the brightest moments of the night. Bryan knew that highlighting Big Sister's work

through those engaged in it should take center stage—to acknowledge all the good work done and all the important work still ahead. The ability to capture the history of an organization and illuminate its continued mission and future importance is a rare gift and one that Bryan thankfully has and shares with causes close to his heart. Over the years, Bryan has worked with MassGeneral Hospital for Children, Boys & Girls Clubs of Boston, Camp Harbor View, the Kennedy Forum on mental health, and many others, some of whose work and events you will read about in this book.

During President Obama's time in the White House, Bryan helped plan different events to showcase the best of our country. When my mom was Secretary of State, she suggested Bryan embrace what she called "design and diplomacy" as a framework for conveying respect and honor to visiting dignitaries through the design of events alongside more traditional diplomacy. Working with the diplomats and other professionals at the State Department and the White House, Bryan created spaces that celebrated the diversity of the countries meeting and set the stage—or table—for a productive discourse. Through the design-and-diplomacy paradigm, Bryan planned lunches at the State Department and state dinners at the White House, including for visiting heads of state from Japan, the United Kingdom, Italy, and Germany. The last included a dramatic moment as Bryan had planned for the first open-air state dinner in the Rose Garden and then worried about the weather—to find out what happened, you'll have to read the story on page 208!

Bryan has spent his life creating memorable, special, and truly unique moments through his events. As a bride, granddaughter, advocate, and citizen, I am grateful he has chosen to share his talents, imagination, and heart in the way he has. I hope this book only marks his life and impact so far, as I know he has so much more to give.

INTRODUCTION

I have the best job in the world.

Twenty-three years ago, I started out with a business card and an idea. Things have evolved, of course, but the idea has remained the same: I help organizations, families, and individuals celebrate the events that matter most to them. I don't believe there is a single recipe for success, but I've learned to rely on some key ingredients: passion combined with efficiency, strategy with originality, design with detail. Today, as one of the nation's premier event planners, we create, design, and execute almost seventy-five events per year across the country and around the world.

I believe every celebration should be unique, a reflection of who you are. It should tell your story. The most memorable celebrations are created by surprising guests and taking them on a journey of unexpected twists. And while it's always nice to have a big budget to spend, often smart, simple tricks offer the most compelling transformations. In this book, I've gathered some of my favorite events: weddings, charity galas, anniversary celebrations, and birthday parties (even my own!). I've also included some of my work at the White House. These pages show off many of my favorite techniques for planning a memorable party, and I hope they'll provide you with inspiration for throwing your own.

After all, it's my job to help you make your celebration unforgettable.

In retrospect, I was preparing for this job my whole life.

I grew up in a big, happy New England family. My mother is very creative, and she loved to decorate. Our kitchen had snow-white cabinets, red checked wallpaper on the cabinet door inserts, and a big wall covered in blue-and-red bandanna-patterned wallpaper. Mom knew she needed a red refrigerator to complete the space, but they didn't make one in those days. So she had my dad take our refrigerator to an auto-parts place, where they painted it fire-engine red. I always tell my team that anything is possible, and I mean it. Think about that refrigerator.

My mother and father loved to throw parties. Every achievement and milestone called for a celebration. If my sister Toni got an A in school, my mother and I would decorate a cake in the shape of an A that night, with a candle for Toni to blow out. If my brother Kerry won a track meet, he got brand-new sneakers filled with malted-milk balls in the team's colors, also complete with a candle. Every celebration was unique to each of us.

Holidays were big, too—literally. Everything was about abundance. On Memorial Day, all of our relatives would come together for a huge barbecue: hamburgers, hot dogs, and Italian sausages, with hundreds of mini American flags and lawn games. On St. Patrick's Day, my father would take a bottle of green food coloring and create an epic party: green milk, green orange juice, green eggs, and his specialty, green pancakes. Christmas meant trees upon trees, multiple gingerbread houses, scores of elves, and Santas on every shelf and table. My mother loves pink, and one year she found an antique sled to put on the front lawn, which we filled with pink-wrapped packages topped with pink bows. She always made Christmas her own.

As much as I love putting on events, it took me a little while to realize that it was what I wanted to do professionally.

I studied political science in college because I wanted to change the world. After college, I took a job at Filene's, the legendary Boston department store, as an assistant buyer in the china, crystal, and silver department. I decided to go back to school for design, and then I went to work at an architecture firm that specialized in high-end bank interiors. It wasn't a conscious plan, but I was developing professional expertise in, first, the things that create a beautiful table and, second, the things that make a sophisticated but functional room. Without meaning to, I was setting myself up for my eventual career.

This was in the mid-1980s, and when a close friend was diagnosed with HIV/AIDS, everything changed. I spent weeks at his family's home as he got sicker. I met Larry Kessler, the executive director of the AIDS Action Committee, who made frequent house calls to the family. Larry became a compassionate mentor to me, and after my friend's death, he told me it was time to turn my pain into action and become a volunteer.

So I did. I joined AAC's events committee, and I started learning about the world of fundraising and galas. At first, I volunteered for event registration and set things up and broke them down. I solicited items for silent auctions and designed signs and invitations. I learned more as I went along, and I discovered I had a real knack for it. Soon, I was executing events big and small. I'd found a way to combine my talents, my training, and my desire to make a difference. I'd found my calling.

I became chair of the events committee, orchestrating six or eight events a year, including danceathons, walkathons, and black-tie galas. To be successful fundraisers, they all needed to be compelling. I learned the importance of creating memorable images and special moments; I learned the importance of telling a story. By 1993, Larry told me I should be getting paid for what I was doing. That's when I started my own company—with the AIDS Action Committee as my first client.

A few years later, I was asked to design Boston's annual Festival of Trees, a fundraiser at which twenty-five designers decorate holiday trees to raise money for the Boston Children's Hospital League. The committee had heard about my work, and they asked me for ideas. I'd seen pictures of previous events, which had hundreds of people attending in one room, making it hard to see the trees.

When I met the client in the hotel lobby where the party would be held, I made my pitch. High planter boxes surrounded the room, and I wanted to cover them with plywood and place the trees on top. They loved the idea, and I had the job. I'd also discovered one of my principles: shoulders and above. What matters in designing an event, I realized then and always emphasize now, is how a room looks when it's full and what people can see around and above all the other guests.

My biggest break came in 1996. Beth Israel Deaconess Medical Center was set to host its annual benefit at the Copley Place shopping center, in Boston's Back Bay neighborhood. This was a high-profile charity event that drew all of the area's most prominent philanthropists. I was asked to produce a dinner for 1,300 guests inside the shopping gallery. The big impact moment was an installation of twelve 100-foot-long metallic ribbons in five colors dangling in the center's atrium. They were inspired by the ribbons you see on gifts, the kind you can curl with a pair of scissors. People loved them; the way the metallic ribbons twirled in the natural airflow was a delightful and memorable surprise for the guests, visible from anywhere in the gallery. That moment formulated another of my guiding principles: an amazingly simple idea can take on a life of its own.

This was exactly what I'd always wanted to be doing. I had used my skills to put on a great event for a great organization, and I helped them raise a lot of money. And there was a side benefit: one of the couples on the host committee asked me what other fundraisers I was working on. I mentioned that I was helping to raise money for a van for a homeless shelter. "No problem," they said. "We'll buy the van." That's when a flash really went off—by working with people who had the means to support major charities, I'd make connections that could help support other organizations I cared about.

The Beth Israel Deaconess event was such a success that the cochairs asked me to plan their daughter's wedding. I wasn't sure I could give them the wedding they were looking for, but they were certain. "This is what you're doing, Bryan," they said. "You're creating memorable experiences. That's what a great wedding is." And they were right. Today, I like to say that I have the honor of getting married more than a dozen times each year; celebrating the romance of each couple truly is a labor of love.

Whether we are designing weddings, anniversaries, state dinners, or a World Series Championship party, we are celebrating people's stories.

I helped project a rainbow on the front of the White House to celebrate marriage equality. I've opened up grand houses to raise millions for the Boys & Girls Clubs. I built a ballroom floating on a barge in a harbor. And my clients have become friends: for one family, I designed a gorgeous sixty-fifth-anniversary party at the Rainbow Room in New York City, followed only a year later by a totally different but equally special Hamptons wedding for their granddaughter.

In fact, this special family introduced me to a U.S. president and his wife, who also happened to be a senator from New York—and eventually the secretary of state and then the first woman to be a major party's presidential nominee. Meeting the Clintons, and designing and planning their daughter Chelsea's wedding, led to a relationship with yet another First Family, the Obamas, who tapped us to design more than a dozen events at the White House, including state dinners and the annual White House holiday decorations.

In the pages that follow, I'll take you inside some of these events, and I'll explain my principles of how to throw a great party. But I also want you to remember that it's never *just* a party. Whether it's an under-the-stars state dinner in the White House Rose Garden or a family meal on St. Patrick's Day, every celebration should tell a story.

Let me tell you those stories, so you can begin writing your own.

PART I

The Perfect Celebration Is Your Celebration

The perfect celebration is a beautiful idea. Designing it, however, can be overwhelming. There is no secret formula to getting it right. Every person and couple is unique, and so is every design. A celebration succeeds when passion is combined with originality, attention is paid to details, a surprise or two is added, and everyone, especially the guest of honor, has fun.

This is particularly important for a wedding. Traditions matter, but you can reinterpret them. Think about the story of your relationship and how you can tell it through the ceremony's location, decor, or food. We have helped clients get married on a sprawling horse ranch in Aspen, Colorado; say their vows under thousands of pieces of confetti; and throw the bouquet from the balcony of a palace in Istanbul. Every wedding should tell a couple's unique story. I hope the following stories inspire you to tell your own.

THERE'S NO PLACE
LIKE HOME

Every American family wants to see their daughter married in her hometown. It's even better when she met her husband there, and her family still lives nearby. But the challenge can be to create a unique wedding in a place you know so well.

This couple loved Boston, and they knew they wanted to get married by the water, in a garden, with a view of the city. Because it was practically impossible to attain all three with one location, I recommended that the couple consider a change of scenery between the ceremony and the reception. Such a change is often a wonderful way to add drama to an event.

We began the night in high style: the ceremony was held in the glorious European-style courtyard of the Boston Public Library, a Beaux Arts masterpiece designed by Charles Follen McKim that opened in 1895. Often our event design is inspired by the architectural details of the venue, from stationery to the shapes of dining tables to the wedding canopy itself. Here, we replicated the beautiful arches of McKim's courtyard in the shape and scale of the chuppah. Guests were seated all around the courtyard, in its grand walkways and the balconies above (I thought those were the best seats!). I prefer to seat guests in several places, rather than in one big group, to give different experiences of the ceremony to the guests.

Dinner and dancing were to follow on the Boston waterfront, but where? Once we determined the perfect spot didn't exist, we convinced the family to build their very own wedding location. We constructed a barge with everything we needed: a dinner tent with real glass windows, a two-tiered oval dining room, a state-of-the-art chef's kitchen, all the power and water necessary, and a beautiful outdoor garden with a view of both the water and the city beyond.

When the big day came, we sailed the barge to a marina that boasted a spectacular water view of the harbor on one side and, on the other, a magical view of the city the couple loved.

PREVIOUS PAGE: A bride and her parents entered the Boston Public Library for her wedding. OPPOSITE: Hundreds of brightly colored dahlias assembled into one mass formed a distinctive swirl against the vast green lawn.

THE REHEARSAL DINNER

I f you are fortunate enough to have an endless green lawn and epic tree in your backyard, I highly recommend hosting one of your wedding events at home. You'll always be able to look out at that verdant landscape and have a priceless memory of a magical night.

We were excited to create an at-home rehearsal dinner at the bride's family's magnificent property. Inspiration was everywhere, from the massive emerald lawn to the classic New England family home. The client had also constructed a beautiful bleached-wood boardwalk that floated above the ground cover and cut through a grove of exceptionally tall trees, opening onto that perfectly manicured lawn. The shape of the walkway offered a beautiful rhythm to the celebration, and it inspired the massive black and white–striped dining table that seated 125 guests.

The grounds of the house were pristine and all in shades of green—bushes, grasses, trees—with not a flower anywhere. This gave us a great canvas on which to use hundreds of multicolored dahlias spilling onto that perfect lawn. The bright flower swirl, in the shape of the table and walkway, was like a statement necklace on a simple black dress.

LEFT: The curve of the flowers echoed the shape of the dining table, which itself mirrored the walkway through the woods that guests used to enter the party. OPPOSITE: Mixing white and black dining chairs in an irregular pattern made the long dining table stand out even more.

LEFT: Dahlias on the tabletop complemented the huge arrangement of dahlias on the lawn.
OPPOSITE: Black water goblets and playful accents of magentas, pinks, black, and white created a contemporary movement down the tablescape.

THE CEREMONY AND RECEPTION

When a wedding happens in several locations, you get to make many different visual statements. This wedding, with so many iconic moments, was a fantastic example of that.

Upon arriving at this neoclassical building, guests were greeted by a stunning marble staircase covered in ivy and candlelight. Hundreds of votive candles twinkled on every available surface, setting the stage for the guests' journey to the open-air courtyard where the ceremony was held. A gurgling fountain accompanied the string quartet playing from the courtyard's Juliet balcony as the wedding party processed through the grounds to the stunning floral chuppah. After the ceremony, to the guests' surprise, we took them all down to the harbor in classic white trolleys. Celebrations are most memorable when things are unexpected, and any kind of surprise helps, whether it's a moment, a visual element, or, in this case, the entire reception venue.

As guests approached the waterfront and prepared to board the barge, they entered a tunnel of greenery we had created for a dramatic arrival moment. Whenever possible, we like to have guests enter a big space from a smaller, more intimate one. Starting small makes that transition to the larger space so much more striking. It frames the view guests see as they walk toward the entrance, elevating their anticipation of what's to come. When they enter the big space, it's almost like another surprise.

The facade of the Boston Public Library boasts some of the most spectacular Beaux Arts architecture in America, a fine backdrop for a wedding designed to celebrate the bride's hometown.

OPPOSITE: The bronze sculpture of a female nude in the library's courtyard was controversial when first placed there in 1896. Today, it makes a beautiful centerpiece.
LEFT: The chuppah, formed from the blooms and stems of white delphiniums, larkspurs, and stocks, echoed the arches of the building's colonnade.

LEFT, CLOCKWISE FROM TOP LEFT: A combination of spray roses, garden roses, and South American rose varietals lined the entry to the reception on a custom-fitted barge. The cake, by legendary designer Sylvia Weinstock, on display. A living rose wall, through which the guests entered; tropical ti leaves were added to the wall to evoke a sense of motion.
OPPOSITE: Guests, greeted by waiters offering champagne, entered under a canopy of English ivy, with the cake framed in the distance.

LEFT: Chandeliers of white wisteria swayed with the movement of the floating dining room.
OPPOSITE: For centerpieces on the oversize tables, calla lilies, lady's slipper orchids, Veronica flowers, and seasonal grasses were arranged in the Japanese ikebana style, an understated foil to a room surrounded by thousands of roses and variegated leaves.
FOLLOWING PAGES: The floating dining room on a barge, with the Boston skyline in the distance.

AN OTTOMAN AFFAIR

The first time I met this family, I knew they would have a cherished place in my heart. The bride was raised in Texas, but her mother's family comes from Turkey. Throughout her childhood, she and her brother spent idyllic summers with their grandparents in Istanbul, weaving themselves into the ancient cultural fabric there. Although she loved her time abroad, when it came time to plan her wedding, a U.S.-based celebration seemed to be the only thing that made sense—the vast majority of her friends and family lived here. So the couple began to envision all that their wedding might be right here at home.

Fate has a way of changing our carefully laid plans, however. When planning got underway, the bride realized her 94-year-old Turkish grandmother wouldn't be able to make the journey. She and her family decided to bring the wedding to Istanbul, to demonstrate their love for her grandmother and to seize the chance to show off this special place for their American friends.

My task was to put together a flawless wedding weekend that not only included sumptuous dinners and a gorgeous ceremony and reception, but also showcased a place that meant so much to this family. The capital city of four different empires, Istanbul has a rich history and culture that reflect its embrace of both the European and Asian continents. We wanted everyone to love Istanbul as much as the bride did.

We began with Istanbul's abundant past, planning a series of events at historical locations across the city. The Bosporus, the natural waterway that separates the two continents and divides the city, became our highway—and I mean that literally. Traffic in Istanbul in August is terrible, so we engaged a fleet of boats to transport guests all weekend. It was a pragmatic solution that also happened to be incredibly romantic.

Opening night was the rehearsal dinner, in a half-decrepit yet gorgeously preserved Ottoman palace. An all-invited welcome dinner the following night was a tribute to Turkish culture that we staged in a grand, historic underground cistern. The finale was the wedding, and no location was more suitable than a magnificent and perfectly restored nineteenth-century white-marble palace overlooking the water. We took their guests on a literal journey that showed off the city, highlighted its past, and embraced the couple's future.

A hanging garden of wisteria, vanda orchids, hydrangeas, olive branches, English ivy, bougainvillea, and hanging amaranthus took seventy-two hours to install. Mirrored tabletops helped to show it off.

THE REHEARSAL DINNER

The Esma Sultan Mansion was built in the late 1800s for an Ottoman princess. After the collapse of the empire, it fell into disrepair; a warehouse for a while, it was gutted by fire in the 1970s. Today, it's a beautiful open space, with the exterior ruins preserved and a glass shell inserted inside that has transformed it into a stunning place for a party. It's also filled with meaning: surrounded by a church, a synagogue, and a mosque, it echoes the blending of the bride's and groom's families. Positioned under the famous First Bridge connecting the European and Asian sides of Istanbul, the palace was a symbol of the passage to the couple's new life. And, of course, the Ottoman sultans were known for their lavish, torchlit parties every night.

When we first visited the palace, the bride's family told me that at those Ottoman parties, live turtles with candles affixed to their backs would wander freely, illuminating the palace with ever-changing patterns of light. To evoke this bygone era, we filled the palace with candles, using more than one hundred handmade crystal-and-silver candlesticks, inspired by one I saw on a visit to the Grand Bazaar. There were reflective surfaces to complement the glass walls, such as mirrored tabletops, glass chairs, and silver plates. Finally, when the guests left, walking past an open-air shelf of votives and toward the twinkling Bosporus, we gave each one a small silver turtle as a souvenir of a night to remember.

RIGHT: The exterior walls of the Esma Sultan Mansion are webbed with vines. We added the wall of votive candles, to bring flickering candlelight outside. FOLLOWING PAGES: Our hanging garden turned an unadorned ceiling into something beautiful, and echoed the bougainvillea vines on the outside of the building.

TOP LEFT: Silver turtle candleholders harkened back to an old Ottoman tradition. BOTTOM LEFT AND OPPOSITE: We used silver and crystal in candlesticks, tabletops, and chairs to echo the modern glass-and-steel structure inside the palace's old walls.

THE WELCOME DINNER

There's an energy and intensity to Istanbul, an amazing city at the crossroads of myriad cultures—so many sights, sounds, smells, and tastes. This evening was our chance to put this remarkable place on display for 380 guests, and we wanted to showcase all of it.

The Binbirdirek Cistern, built in the fourth century, is one of the oldest underground water reservoirs in the world. It's magnificent and was the perfect setting for the welcome dinner. I firmly believe that you should study a great city or historic venue carefully and create a design that respectfully pays tribute to its key attributes, rather than trying to replicate it whole. We took the plain cement entryway and covered it with Ottoman rugs, lit it with Turkish lanterns—all things we found at the Grand Bazaar, only a few hundred feet away from Binbirdirek—and even built a laser-cut false wall with a Byzantine pattern to make the entry hall grander in scale.

Inside, we wanted to give the feeling of abundance you experience at the bazaar. Pushcarts were filled with roses and spices. Escort cards rested in sacks overflowing with pomegranate seeds and ground spices. The food was local meze—fresh vegetables, spiced meats, and stuffed grape leaves—served small plate–style so you could taste a little of everything. We even had whirling dervishes perform, members of the Mevlevi Order who go into an almost trancelike state when they dance. It wasn't a theme party; it was the essence of the culture.

RIGHT: Heavy drapes, Turkish lanterns, and thousands of scattered rose petals made for a dramatic entrance to the welcome dinner at the Binbirdirek Cistern. FOLLOWING PAGES: We rented rugs at the Grand Bazaar to warm up the cement hall, and we built the Byzantine-style false wall at its end to create intimacy.

40

LEFT AND OPPOSITE: The Grand Bazaar, only a few hundred yards from Binbirdirek, overflows with things to browse and buy. We filled baskets and bags to convey a similar abundance. FOLLOWING PAGES: We created a beautiful, classically Ottoman reception inside the historic cistern. Thin white ropes pulled tight from the ceiling toward receptacles on the floor drew dripping water out of the way.

LEFT: Dozens of fresh orchid strands form a striking ceiling installation over an ancient water well below, hidden from view by the surrounding custom teal velvet sofas. In such a grand space, a mix of traditional ballroom chairs, upholstered dining chairs, and upholstered love seats created intimate dining experiences. OPPOSITE: Many of the pieces we used, like the hammered-brass cloches on the tables, were made for us by Turkish artisans.

LEFT: The whirling dervishes performed the sama, a religious dance that represents a spiritual journey through love and the mind to perfection. OPPOSITE, CLOCKWISE FROM TOP RIGHT: The lighting, custom made for us, was inspired by the pendant luminaries I saw everywhere in Istanbul. Street vendors swirled melted sugar into hard candies that the guests could eat.

THE CEREMONY AND RECEPTION

The Çırağan Palace was crafted from white marble in the mid-1800s for Sultan Abdülâziz, right on the banks of the Bosporus. It's a fairy-tale castle, and the view was breathtaking as the bride arrived in her dazzling gown.

Everyone arrived by boat. A receiving line of footmen was waiting, serving champagne and handing out ceremony programs from silver trays. We designed their outfits, based on old Turkish military uniforms, to make for a remarkable first impression. Guests proceeded to a lawn outside the palace, which we built over a marble courtyard. We erected a truss system overhead, and we hung wisteria that gently waved in the breeze coming off the water. No tent here—you wouldn't want to obstruct the views of the palace, the Bosporus, and the iconic First Bridge.

The bride's vision for her wedding day was a secret garden on the water, reminiscent of the impeccably formal gardens of Paris. So we began with the emerald-green grass and the luminescent gray and white marble of the palace. Then we added layer upon layer of trellised white flowers, creating a canopy under which the guests dined. The gray textiles anchored a stunning tableau in that outdoor ballroom we built overlooking the river, creating perfect views and an intimacy that belied the size of the group. At the end of the evening, the groom gave a toast thanking the families, and then we launched fireworks over the river. The fireworks were a surprise for the bride—and a moment of pure joy for the guests.

The bride and her father entered the ceremony by walking down a 120-foot marble terrace. The palm trees shaded guests— and also offered a beautiful interplay of light and shadow.

PREVIOUS PAGES, LEFT: More than a dozen stone urns overflowing with flowers lined a staircase to the ceremony and made an extraordinary first impression. PREVIOUS PAGES, RIGHT: The bride and groom arrived as their guests did, by sailing up the Bosporus. LEFT: Guests were greeted by rows of waiters in military-inspired uniforms we designed. OPPOSITE, CLOCKWISE FROM TOP LEFT: The attendees were serenaded by violins. Ivy and roses decorate the ceremony seating. Waiters presented guests with programs. The proud father escorted his daughter down the aisle.

PREVIOUS PAGES: Dinner was on a three-level terrace we built overlooking the Bosporus, with hanging wisteria overhead.

LEFT AND OPPOSITE: The table flowers included English ivy, green roses, white and green Dutch hydrangeas, and trick dianthus. Five-layer paper menu cards sat atop custom-made sterling silver chargers.

THE AFTER-PARTY

A great after-party is the sign of a great wedding. When people are having fun, they don't want it to end. And that's especially true at a destination wedding.

When we plan an after-party, we want it to be an absolute juxtaposition to the wedding, so everything feels fresh and new. In this case, we wanted a contrast to the stately elegance of the wedding reception. So we invited the guests inside the palace, up a marble staircase, and then down a sexy, glittering hallway into a sleek European nightclub that we'd created.

A great after-party needs to have some sort of wow moment every twenty minutes or so, because it's late and you have to keep the energy going. That can be a music shift, a confetti blast, or incredible dancers. The best wow moment here happened early. When guests entered, it was like they were coming into a luxurious lounge with plush couches, a mirrored bar, and pulsing music. Then once everyone was in the room, the amazing DJ kicked up the beat. A false wall dropped. Behind it was the bride, ready for her big reveal in a sparkly beaded after-party dress. She was the queen of this golden, glittering wonderland.

PREVIOUS PAGES: A surprise fireworks display capped off the reception. RIGHT: For the after-party, guests moved inside to the glittering nightclub we designed.

64

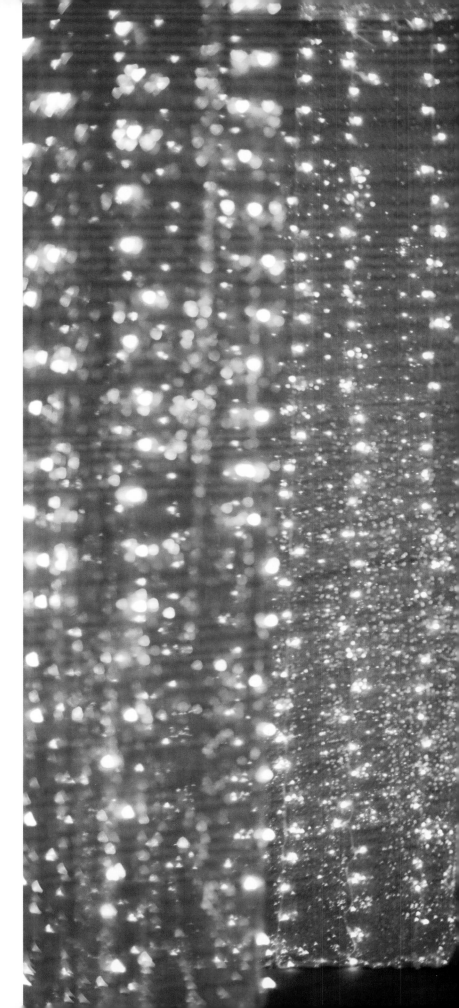

There can never be too many mirrored surfaces in a nightclub, so we spray-painted palm leaves gold and placed them in gold reflective vases. The walls and windows were covered with black velvet, with gold drape embedded with twinkle lights layered on top of that. FOLLOWING PAGES: It's hard to believe that this sleek club was created inside the centuries-old Çırağan Palace.

COMING HOME

We firmly believe that the perfect wedding celebration, no matter where it's held, should reflect the couple and their families—their sensibilities, histories, and story. We create a moment in time when guests feel as if the wedding couple has invited them into their home and family. Finding that perfect union of intimacy and warmth is one of my favorite parts of being in this business.

So imagine our delight when this couple decided to host their wedding at their beautiful new home, surrounded by their closest family and friends.

The bride and groom were both established professionals who had moved cities to be together, and part of their bond was in making this property their mutual home. It was obvious from our first visit that this was a labor of love, and that hosting their wedding here was their way of showing their passion for one another and their future life together. The combination of their love for the history of the place, once a working vineyard, and the personal stamp they'd put on it—by raising more than twenty alpacas—was something we simply had to let shine through on their wedding day.

Once we ascertained that no room in the house could accommodate all their guests for dinner, we decided to build a tent that would be an extension of their home. We chose a tent with an eave-end roof to complement the house, and the formality of the brass fixtures and chandeliers set the scene for the black-tie reception the bride had dreamed of. Wrapping the tent uprights in the same lattice treatment seen on the grounds made the tent appear integrated with the home and served as a natural transition outdoors. We kept the palette to the hues of the stunning property—greens and whites, with a touch of taupe and sand to enhance the fieldstone walls.

We often say to a bride who isn't sure if she wants to get married at her parents' house, "Imagine years from now that you'll have children running around, and you'll be able to say to them, 'This is where mommy and daddy got married.'"

This couple believed in that idea. They built their house for it. Their wedding said, "We're building this life together, and we want you to be a part of it."

OPPOSITE: Dramatic arrangements of pear branches, delphiniums, native conical hydrangeas, Dutch hydrangeas, and an assortment of spray and garden roses, all in a palette of greens, whites, and taupe, suited the stunning property. FOLLOWING PAGES: The eaved, glass-walled wedding tent complemented the home the couple built together and contrasted pleasantly with the fieldstone garden walls.

TOP LEFT: An assortment of native greens, hydrangeas, and roses ornamented the backs of the ceremony seating.

BOTTOM LEFT: We adorned sculptures on the property for the celebration.

OPPOSITE: Escort cards were placed atop a cornucopia of grapes, reflecting the property's past as a vineyard.

FOLLOWING PAGES: The tent, with columns wrapped in French treillage.

The bride found the fabric for the tablecloths, a beautiful heavy silk with a brocaded design, on her travels in China. The brass candelabras and chandeliers made the tented ballroom feel like an extension of the house.

ALL-AMERICAN ELEGANCE

The great American West, with its epic vistas and beautiful red sunsets, is a canvas I have long wanted as a backdrop. When our bride came to us and said her family's most special memories and experiences were made during their trips out West, I could not have been more excited.

We have certain key principles for a destination wedding. Chief among them is our desire to celebrate and complement the true spirit of the breathtaking surroundings at the chosen destination. In this case, that meant we would use the best assets of a 30,000-acre working cattle ranch, while being thoughtful about the couple and their family to create a personal wedding story that really reflected them.

The welcome dinner and rehearsal dinner were combined into one occasion. We scouted the ranch and landed on a horse-riding arena. Because it was a working ranch, the arena was filled with the tools of its trade, not to mention horses and row upon row of hay bales. One of our core principles in any venue setting is to take stock of our assets, so that's where we began. We built our design around the horse trailers and hay bales. Those hay bales became lounge furniture, while the horse trailer became a fitting foreground for the giant American-flag backdrop that rose front and center. And the horses were invited to the party.

We took every opportunity to create an authentic narrative between our couple and their love for this particular property. We built a giant arch surrounding the entrance to the arena, with 500 individual cowboy hats—which we made removable so that guests could put them on during the party. A curated barbecue menu fit our surroundings perfectly—and, as an added bonus, the deliciously scented smoke helped dull the natural smells of the ranch! Fitting the family-style, down-home atmosphere, the guests gathered around long tables and sipped drinks from jelly jars. And what's a cattle-ranch party without a brand? We created a custom brand mark for our couple, and we stamped it on everything from the signs at the buffet to place mats to napkin rings—with, because we just couldn't help ourselves, a mini cowbell tied to each one.

OPPOSITE: An archway made up of hundreds of red-ribboned cowboy hats set against foraged seasons green leaves formed an unexpected entryway. The red ribbons connected to our red, white, and blue theme. FOLLOWING PAGES: Hay-bale walls and a giant American flag helped scale down a cavernous horse arena, creating warmth and an intimate party space.

We dressed the tables in red, white, and blue, with flower arrangements of locally foraged wild grasses and herbs, which added a nostalgic fragrance to the experience.

LEFT: Everything was branded with the couple's initials, including kraft-paper place mats and red cowbells. Guests rang the bells during the toasts.
OPPOSITE: We repurposed a horse trailer found in the arena as part of our design, made the cowboy hats accessible, so that guests could take them off the arch and wear them, and used the couple's brand everywhere.

STOPPING TIME

During the design and planning of a wedding, a couple can never supply enough inspirational content to me and my team. I always ask the brides and grooms to bring it on: Pinterest, Instagram, mood boards. So many couples have no idea what they want; trying to express who you are and what you want to evoke at your wedding can feel insurmountable.

I often tell clients that wedding planning is like boot camp: you challenge your intuitions and build trust in each other. You begin to understand who each of you is—separately and together. You learn to express yourself as a couple, as two families coming together for a lifetime.

From the outset, this bride and groom were perfectly matched. After college, they created their own Brooklyn-based circus-production company. But even these super-creative kindred spirits had to embark on their own journey of discovery to figure out the wedding they really wanted to have.

A Beaux Arts bank building recently renovated to its original grandeur spoke to them almost immediately as the perfect spot to host their wedding. With its breathtaking ceilings, embossed hinges, and two million imported marble tiles on its rotunda and dome, it was the quintessential location for a couple who spent their days producing the spectacular.

Despite the bride and groom's passion for the theatrical, they also wanted to be thoughtful about celebrating a wedding, not creating another circus performance. The bride's Pinterest page was covered in images of brightly colored flowers, beautiful wedding dresses, incredibly decorative desserts, and lots and lots of confetti. But one thing stood out: a quote that read, "When you fall in love, time stops." When I read that, I saw an opportunity for a wedding inspired by their talent, creativity, and love for each other. Could we stop time?

Whatever we did in that dramatic, cavernous domed space would have to be big. Really big. With the bride's quote in mind, we created a chandelier made of confetti. But the confetti needed to look like it was stopped in midair, just like their lives stopped when they fell in love. It took 28,000 pieces of confetti glued to 1,600 strands of clear fishing line to achieve our goal. A fantastical design that was also refined, the chandelier served as an homage to their love and to their creativity, without turning their wedding into a circus.

OPPOSITE: The central rotunda of a meticulously restored old bank building in the Williamsburg neighborhood of Brooklyn made a stunning location for a wedding ceremony. FOLLOWING PAGES: Later, we converted that same space, still with our confetti explosion overhead, for dinner and dancing.

OPPOSITE: Purple allium blossoms, orange gloriosa lilies, and delicate maidenhair foliage, coupled with mirrored tabletops, created excitement for the escort-card table. RIGHT, CLOCKWISE FROM TOP LEFT: The reception site's exterior. A floating array of oversize, shiny, metallic balls added energy and whimsy to the bank's neoclassical entry. The bride and groom read their vows from his-and-hers notebooks. Carnation spheres echoed the balls' shape and alluded to the idea of eternity.

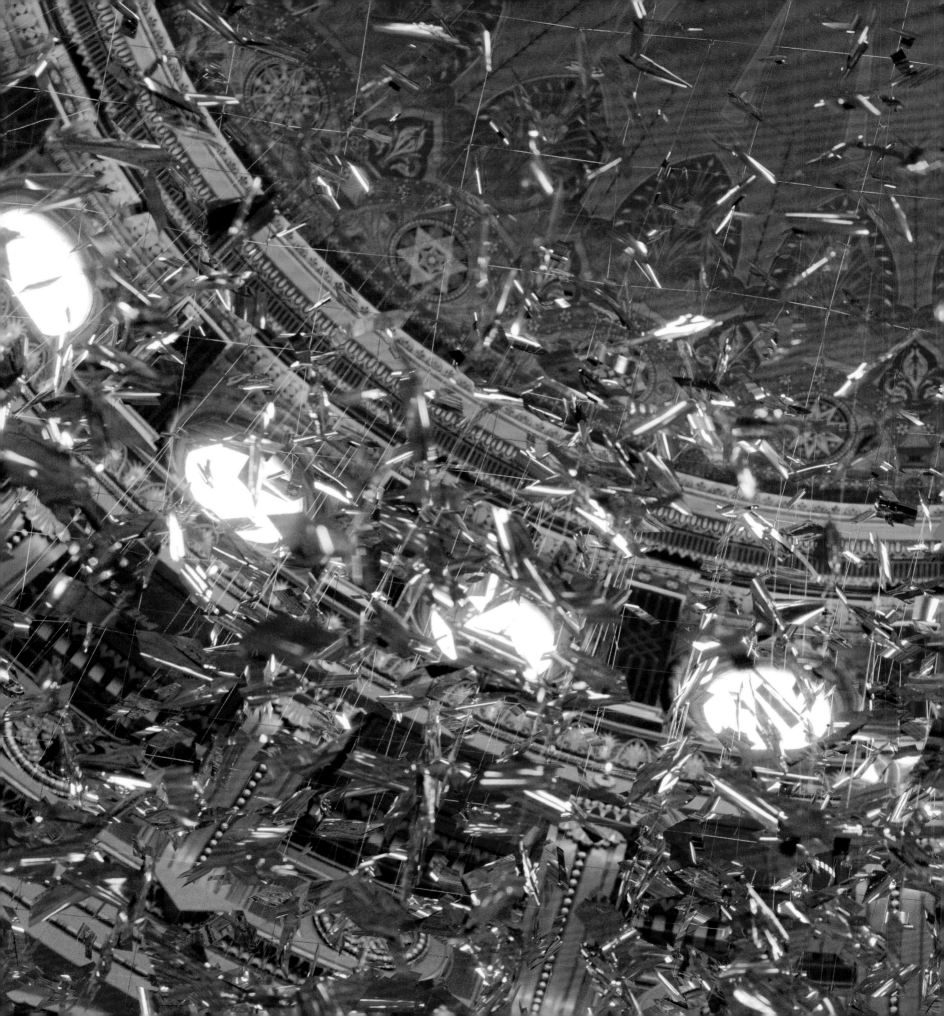

PREVIOUS PAGES: Looking up at the meticulously restored bank dome through the confetti explosion. LEFT AND OPPOSITE: "I cannot believe I had a fuchsia-and-purple wedding," the bride told me later, laughing. The bright colors and mirrored surfaces gave the room an extraordinary energy.

LEFT AND OPPOSITE: I always love to make a statement with multiple small items, especially at a dessert bar, where that kind of abundance gives your guests permission to have one (or more!) of everything.

NO PLACE FOR ORDINARY

As they say in Aspen, "This is no place for ordinary." Our bride's roots in the Rocky Mountains had given her a love for their natural beauty, and she and her groom envisioned a destination wedding in the resort town. They wanted to spend a bit more time with their friends and family, too, so we planned four days of celebrations that would create an ideal chance for their guests to make a vacation of it. Who wouldn't want to spend as much time as possible in the mountains of Colorado?

When guests travel for a destination wedding, investing time and money to be there, they deserve an incredible weekend. I like to start off on a high-energy note. For this wedding, festivities kicked off with a Wild West welcome party held at a friend's barn on Thursday night. Friday was a picnic and lawn games—this couple was playfully competitive, as were their friends—followed by a rehearsal dinner at the iconic Aspen Mountain Club.

The ceremony and wedding dinner were held the next day on a forty-eight-acre ranch covered with field grasses, horse stables, and aspen trees. The couple exchanged vows between a two-and-a-half-acre meadow, with a fully stocked trout pond, and a twenty-stall horse barn. The Rockies provided a dramatic backdrop for the almost 400 guests in attendance. The focal point for the ceremony was an olive branch–laden floral arch covered in almost a dozen different varieties of peach, rose, pink, and green flowers. It did a beautiful job of intimately framing the couple against the panoramic mountain view beyond.

The wedding dinner was held in a perfectly appointed 17,500-square-foot indoor riding arena. Our design challenge was to create an intimate dining room for the guests while celebrating this magnificent horse cathedral. We were lucky enough to be able to suspend a beautiful floral ceiling of wisteria in shades ranging from light pink to deeper burgundy from the 200-foot-long steel rods that support the barn. We used restaurant-size banquet seating and upholstered dining chairs to add to the scale of the structure.

To top it all off, dinner was accompanied by a twenty-five-piece orchestra on a two-tiered stage—with all of the musicians sporting white dinner jackets, of course. Tributes to each family's heritage, Irish and Colombian, were woven throughout the reception—especially when it came to the music.

The bride's bouquet at this lovely outdoor wedding complemented the
muted tones of the flowers in the monumental wedding arch.

The couple was married between a meadow, with a fully stocked trout pond, and a classic horse barn. FOLLOWING PAGES: The wedding arch, built of olive branches and more than a dozen varieties of flowers, served as a counterpoint to the vast expanse of the Rocky Mountains in the background.

LEFT: The wedding aisle was flanked by flower boxes filled with native grasses and wildflowers. OPPOSITE, CLOCKWISE FROM TOP LEFT: A printed program becomes a commemorative record of your wedding day. Bridal bouquets gathered varietals of pink astilbes, seeded eucalyptuses, and silver dusty millers. A sea of bleached-wood cross-back chairs complemented Aspen's mountains.

To construct an intimate dining room inside this vast horse barn, we built a floral ceiling made from faux wisteria. Upholstered dining chairs complemented the scale of the imposing room.

OPPOSITE, CLOCKWISE
FROM TOP LEFT: The barn
door at night. The bride
and her brothers
celebrating on stage. An
understated wedding cake
sat quietly amid the
opulent room design.
Mirrored tables and silver
chargers reflected the
hanging garden above.
RIGHT: Tall candlesticks
added height to the
table and complemented
the scale of the room.

SYMBOLISM IN SOHO

This stylish Manhattan couple chose a SoHo loft for their wedding, a fitting backdrop for the incredibly creative story they had to tell. One groom is an actor, and the other is an activist. They wanted to get married in New York, they said, to support the state that was supportive of their union. The grooms had founded a tie company, Tie the Knot, whose mission is to advocate for civil rights for gay and lesbian Americans throughout the United States and beyond.

To show off this couple's eclecticism and to speak to the connections and diversity underlying the whole event, we suggested using different kinds of seating for the ceremony—vintage church pews, wooden chairs, and iron garden chairs in different patterns, shapes, and colors. We also created a wall with framed photos of their friends and family and the history of their courtship, plus drawings and other artwork. And we fashioned the couple an oversize monogram out of old spools of thread, which hangs in their home on the West Coast today.

The more a couple can share with us about the things they love and why, the deeper the connections we can create for family and friends attending the wedding. In a long conversation the first time we met, the grooms mentioned their love for antique keys and their affection for Edison bulbs. They also said lots of kids would be attending with their parents, and they wanted to be sure they felt included. Keeping this in mind, we rounded up dozens of old keys and used them for escort cards—"your key to the party," we called them. We hung Edison bulbs above a Bourbon bar, mimicking the look of their favorite restaurant. And for the guest book, we created a simple watercolor station with an invitation to guests to make little paintings with memories or hopes for the grooms. It was conceived as something for the kids to do, but it grew into an inspiring opportunity for all the artists and writers in the room to honor their hosts.

The result was a union of imagination and love to last a lifetime.

The grooms and their guests paraded through the streets of New York City's SoHo to the after-party.

LEFT: A wide variety of different seating styles for the ceremony underscored the diversity and inclusivity of the grooms' lives and activism. OPPOSITE: Instead of a wedding arch or a chuppah, we created a wedding canopy made from 300 yards of cotton muslin, cut into pieces ranging from 4 inches to 5 feet wide.

OPPOSITE: A memory wall filled with photographs of the grooms' courtship.

RIGHT, CLOCKWISE FROM TOP LEFT: Because the grooms love antique keys, escort cards were guests' "key to the party." Custom cocktail coasters announced that the grooms were officially married. A monogram we made from old bobbins of thread; it now hangs in their Los Angeles home. The custom cake topper, including the couple's Maltese-Yorkie shelter dog, was created by an artist and handmade of paper.

LEFT AND OPPOSITE: We proposed the watercolor station for kids, but during planning it grew into a beautiful, meaningful way for guests to leave messages and memories for the couple. At the end of the evening, we collected the artworks and presented them to the grooms in an elegant box.

WE'RE LOOKIN' FOR A BOX FULL OF ♥ -JL

OPPOSITE: A combination of long and round dining tables, along with crystal chandeliers offset by the loft's cast-iron columns, continued the eclectic feeling.
RIGHT: European-style gathered arrangements brought together variegated hostas, seasonal berries, poppy pods, scented geraniums, trick dianthus, and passionflowers.

OPPOSITE: Die-cut menus conveyed the couple's sense of whimsy. RIGHT: Earth tones, greens, and warm woods brought an alfresco dining experience indoors. FOLLOWING PAGES: Accent glassware and seasonal greens also brought color and fragrance into the dining room.

A FIFTH AVENUE MASQUERADE

We love a theme party, but it's not often that we are in a position to consider one for a wedding. So of course we were intrigued to craft a masquerade-themed wedding for this couple.

Understanding that the location would be key to the success of this idea, the couple chose the perfect venue: the Frick Collection in New York City. The stunning residence built for Henry Clay Frick in 1912 now houses a museum known for its world-class collection of old master paintings. An elegant Beaux Arts mansion that runs a full block along Fifth Avenue, the Frick is the sort of place that makes it easy to imagine lavish Gilded Age balls, with ladies dressed in gowns and gentlemen in white tails dancing the night away to a full orchestra.

We always suggest to our clients they create their own interpretation of a tradition, in this case a classic masquerade ball. We drew our inspiration for the night from a myriad of places, including fifteenth-century carnival season in France and the Italian Renaissance festivals of the sixteenth century. The invitation called for black-tie attire and asked the guests to consider wearing masks. To the couple's delight, guest after guest arrived wearing beautiful handmade masks of all shapes and sizes. The guests were truly captivated by the theme, and while many wore masks custom made in New York, a few others wore Venetian masks from their trips to Italy. For those guests who chose not to bring a mask, we provided gold laser-cut versions in case they had a change of heart upon arrival.

Long dining tables decorated with black-crystal candelabras encircled the courtyard of the museum, and dinner chargers made of gold glass provided the perfect complement. Red roses, vanda orchids, and burgundy calla lilies lined the center of the tables, evoking the vibrancy and often darker-hued characteristics of Venetian carnivals.

Like a traditional wedding, a masquerade historically encompassed music and dancing, and often mysterious masked characters in fancy dress would mingle with the guests. Between courses at dinner, a group of Venetian violinists dressed in all black—complete with capes and mask—encircled the room playing lacquered-ebony electric violins. The spectacular collection of the Frick provided the final inspiration and set a perfect backdrop for this one-of-a-kind evening.

The elegant and imposing Frick Collection provided a magnificent backdrop
for a wedding dinner modeled on a classic masquerade ball.

Guests dined at long tables in the colonnade
surrounding the Frick's courtyard.

LEFT: Black crystal candelabras added a glamorous accent to the evening. OPPOSITE, CLOCKWISE FROM TOP LEFT: The evening had a sense of mystery and discovery conveyed by a dramatic tabletop; gold chargers contrasted with black china. A jazz ensemble in all white complemented the black-and-white affair. Scrolling calligraphy on the invitation. Jewel-toned florals enlivened the tablescape.

The pleasure of your company
is requested to
CELEBRATE
the marriage of

Heather McDowell
and
Adam Levin

SATURDAY, SEPTEMBER TENTH
two thousand eleven
at seven o'clock in the evening

The Frick Collection
One East Seventieth Street
NEW YORK CITY

black tie
masquerade

LEFT: Venetian violinists, dressed in all black and playing ebony-lacquered electric violins, entertained the guests between courses. OPPOSITE, CLOCKWISE FROM TOP LEFT: Guests were asked to consider bringing masks, and some bought custom ones abroad. The cake fit the masquerade theme, too. We had gold, laser-cut masks on hand, just in case. The bride was in Oscar de la Renta couture.

SIMPLICITY IN THE HAMPTONS

The Parrish Art Museum sits on a fourteen-acre former tree nursery in the Hamptons town of Water Mill. Inspired by its bucolic setting and the artistic life on Long Island's East End, the museum resembles an elongated, connected double barn. Although the building is quite imposing as you approach it along Montauk Highway, once you walk its length you realize that it is, in fact, a very simple structure.

I had known this bride since she was very young, and I was determined to give this beautiful couple everything they were looking for. A dramatic statement—or, for this wedding, several dramatic statements—was imperative. Our challenge was to create a design that showcased a perfect combination of simplicity and quality, something that projected the beauty of the Hamptons while creating a weekend filled with memories, one that would perfectly reflect these special families.

We love the juxtaposition of using simple materials but then massing them out in quantity, things that at face value are understated yet brought to the next level by sheer numbers. Three hundred wicker chairs made a big impact without being extravagant. We surrounded those chairs with a lush dressing of fern and eucalyptus adorned with delphiniums, roses, asters, and larkspurs that reflected the landscape of the museum property. We also created an abundant walkway for the bride and her wedding party, so it felt like they were walking through actual fields on their way to the chuppah.

We always think about how the bride and groom will look to their guests, but it's equally important to consider what they'll see as they say their vows. This is a tremendous moment, so on one site visit, I walked out to the field and measured exactly where the chuppah would be placed. Then I stopped and imagined the couple standing there. What did they see when they looked back down the aisle? They would be standing under a vintage lace canopy, looking back at their friends and family down the honey-colored sisal aisle runner, surrounded by the field grasses and native wildflowers, with the hundreds of white lanterns we'd hung from airplane wire swaying in the wind. And beyond that, the endless fields of the Hamptons, as they would listen to a jazz quartet playing "Your Smiling Face," by James Taylor, the bride's favorite singer.

Asters, hydrangeas, bay branches, delphiniums, and stocks adorned a seasonal escort-card table that was a perfect preview of the simple but elegant tone of the reception.

THE CEREMONY
AND RECEPTION

We marked the area for cocktails with a floating ceiling made of more than one hundred three-foot-wide white paper lanterns hung on airplane wire. The sheer number of lanterns, their size, and the expanse they covered allowed us to make a big statement with very, very simple materials. They also cast hundreds of circular shadows on the ground, adding to the impact of this understated design.

Dinner was served under the museum's elongated barn ceiling. Here, we used hundreds of yards of classic string lights and garlands of mixed salal and ruscus foliage. The lights and greenery added a sense of warmth and luxury to the dining room. In such a contemporary venue, and with the couples' desire for a classic, elegant wedding, it was important that nothing was too large in scale.

We always consider how we use space and look for elements that can both enhance the architecture and create the feeling we want for the party. In this case, we chose long tables to echo the striking architecture of the elongated barn. Individual glass vases of all shapes and sizes filled with roses, hydrangeas, and lisianthuses in blush, soft yellow, and white enhanced the simplicity of the tabletop design. Everything was classic: the glassware, dinnerware, silverware—even a classic hemstitched napkin tied with a mustard-colored velvet ribbon. Together they gave this couple exactly what they wished for.

LEFT: White paper lanterns hung on airplane wire made a big statement with simple materials. OPPOSITE: The lanterns also created a gorgeous vista for the bride and groom as they looked out from under the chuppah.

Long tables with cane-backed chairs both complemented the barnlike shape of the Parrish Art Museum and evoked the feeling of dining at home with the family.

LEFT, CLOCKWISE FROM
TOP: Embroidered
cream-on-cream linens
with goldenrod velvet
ribbon napkin ties added
to the simple and elegant
tablescape. The long
tables match the
museum's signature
elongated shape. The
invitation featured
elegant taupe writing on
a simple cream card.
OPPOSITE: Timeless gold
and silver accents refined
the tabletop decor.
Etched-glass votives
seemed to glow and catch
the setting sun.

OPPOSITE: Reception florals included an assortment of garden and South American roses, green ruscuses, and white hydrangeas. Right: Hundreds of yards of hanging garlands and classic string lights added warmth and luxury to the outdoor dining area. FOLLOWING PAGES: The twinkling lights and candles bathed the party in an inviting glow.

THE AFTER-PARTY

We love a chance to change the tone as our guests travel the emotional roller coaster of a well-conceived wedding. So, at 11:00 p.m., as the band was winding down, we threw open a big door into the museum so guests could exit the reception and enter a thus-far-unnoticed interior room for the after-party. It felt like they were entering a secret cave, and we made sure everything inside was outrageous. Our bride wanted a tropical theme, so we decked the place out with Mylar drapes, funky lighting, and, of course, a disco ball, all with a touch of tropical.

It was outrageous just to be outrageous, because that's what you need to keep things going after eight hours of getting dressed, taking photos, the ceremony, and then the reception. Guests—and the couple—welcome that jolt of energy. We had Tropicana dancers on stilts, just like you'd find in Las Vegas. We had mini burgers and candy and desserts. Don't get me wrong, people had been having a great time outside at the reception. But when this door opened up just after the band played the last dance and guests could hear our rocking DJ, the explosion of energy was enormous. Our goal was to get everyone revved up again for another hour, but they ended up staying for three more hours. Even the groom's 92-year-old grandmother was out on the dance floor. That's when you know it's a great party.

THIS PAGE AND OPPOSITE: A great after-party is a total break from what's come before, so after the simple elegance of the outdoor dinner, we moved inside to an over-the-top tropical-themed disco, complete with dancers on stilts and sculptures made from tropical flowers and fruits.

SIXTY-FIVE YEARS
AND SHINING

Since its debut in 1934, the iconic Rainbow Room has epitomized quintessential New York glamour, rising sixty-five stories above the landmark Rockefeller Center. The Art Deco ballroom, with its classic old-world charm, was just the right setting to celebrate a landmark sixty-fifth wedding anniversary.

The couple in question were some of my very first clients, and they have become dear friends. Since the first party I did for them almost twenty-five years ago, we've worked together on birthday and housewarming parties, political fundraisers, countless nonprofit galas, and, of course, other anniversary parties. I've designed their grandchildren's bar and bat mitzvahs, and I had the honor to produce their first granddaughter's wedding. I love this family, and it was a tremendous honor to be able to help them celebrate such a momentous occasion—how many couples reach sixty-five years together?

This was a party designed to mark a lifetime of extraordinary experiences shared by two awe-inspiring people who were still very much in love. Their children and grandchildren were in attendance, along with notable friends from around the world. The room was also filled with business titans, inventors, researchers, senators, a speaker of the house, a president, a first lady, and a secretary of state. I knew we had to get this right.

My vision was to honor this remarkable moment and a relationship that has stood the test of time in an important venue that has also stood the test of time. The Rainbow Room is, like the couple, legendary. It's a beautiful space with an unbeatable view of the glittering Manhattan skyline. To complement this view, and the thousands of crystals hung around the room, we used a hundred yards of sparkling linens and 250 crystal ballroom chairs. In a place like the Rainbow Room, you can't upstage the space—you can only work to accentuate it. Finally, we filled the room with hundreds of bright fuchsia phalaenopsis orchids—a passionate, vibrant gesture that reflected the passion and vibrancy of their marriage. Flowers may not last a lifetime, but this celebration proved that true love does.

The Rainbow Room is an icon atop the glittering Manhattan skyline. Thousands of crystals hung throughout the room and in the windows made the views even more spectacular.

OPPOSITE: Calligraphed escort cards were accented by a clean line of candlelight. RIGHT, CLOCKWISE FROM TOP LEFT: Saturated pinks balanced the chic and shimmering blacks. We used purple vanda orchids, fuchsia and pink phalaenopsis orchids, peonies, and assorted roses. The menu cards featured rose lace detailing.

Rectangular tabletop chandeliers, crystal Chiavari chairs, mirrored floral vessels, and curtains of crystal added to the Art Deco glamour of the night.

LEFT: Celebrated cake designer Ron Ben-Israel replicated the clients' favorite flowers on their anniversary cake. OPPOSITE: Black crystal candlesticks and linens embedded with sparkly sequins added a custom look.

FELIZ CUMPLEAÑOS

It's not about where you are, people say, just who you're with. But I think place matters, too. And when it came to a husband who wanted to throw his wife an unforgettable milestone birthday weekend, only the most spectacular "where" would suffice.

We scouted several really special places, all in the category of sun and sand. The birthday girl wanted to keep the vibe laid-back and the spaces intimate; she wanted a party with only her closest friends and family members. And, given the reality of their busy lives, the couple wanted someplace so special, it felt like it was on the other side of the moon—without being on the other side of the globe.

We found a boutique hideaway outside Tulum, Mexico, with only forty-one suites. What better way to keep the weekend intimate than to only have so many rooms available? Originally built as the home of an Italian duchess on the most beautiful beach of the Riviera Maya, the majestic fifty-acre estate managed to feel like a beach house while hitting just the right note for our chic guest of honor.

C is for *celebrate*, and it's also our client's first initial—what an opportunity! For the dinner, we created a giant communal dining table in the shape of a C; it was an impactful yet subtle design element. It also happened to nestle on a little patch of green grass hidden away in the lush palm foliage of the Yucatán jungle creeping toward the beach. Naturally, we wanted to do something fun with all the coconuts lying around. We hand-painted them with the guests' names and affixed one to each guest suite's entry. We also enhanced Mother Nature's near-perfect pineapples by adding a simple splash of color to their leaves.

For the final night of C's birthday weekend, she asked her guests to wear all white. A white party is very elegant, and it was the perfect ending to a weekend on the white-sand beaches of the Riviera Maya.

The C-shaped table paid tribute to the birthday girl's name and to celebrating. It also nestled perfectly on a patch of grass between the jungle and the beach. FOLLOWING PAGES: The weekend ended with a white party just steps from the white-sand beaches of the Yucatán.

OPPOSITE, CLOCKWISE FROM TOP LEFT: What's a birthday party in Mexico without tequila? The design for the weekend was inspired by what was around us; naturally beautiful pineapples got a little boost from neon colors. Coconuts were painted with names to label the guest suites. We found these hand-painted maracas on a site visit to Tulum. RIGHT: Ribbon streamers affixed to bamboo poles danced in the tropical breeze and gave the space a celebratory feel.

Dinner under the palm trees and
tropical stars needed only candlelight
and white phalaenopsis orchids.

PART II

Changing the World

I truly believe that we were put on this earth to make this place better than we found it. That's why a third of the work we do is with nonprofits. I love being able to make a difference, and I love the challenge.

When developing design concepts for our nonprofit clients, we start with their mission statements. Just like with any event, our goal is to create an emotional connection for our guests. But here, when we're raising money and awareness, that emotional connection needs to yield tangible results. How do I create a perfectly curated event that respects a busy donor's time, and that's different, exciting, and inspiring? I want the guests who come to these events to leave saying, "I want to be a part of this."

When that happens, people who need help get it. That's the best feeling in the world.

THE STORYBOOK BALL

Every nonprofit has a story to tell. So when we had an opportunity to create a nonprofit fundraiser that was an *actual* story, we couldn't turn the page fast enough.

MassGeneral Hospital for Children was looking to create a concept for a signature annual fundraiser, and we knew we had to connect our theme to what the hospital does—save children's lives. In order to tell the hospital's story, we turned to classic children's stories, using levity and nostalgia to draw the attention of our guests to the children their donations help every day.

Twenty years later, we are still going strong. From that first event, featuring the classic book *The Trumpet of the Swan*, our sophistication has grown in leaps and bounds. I recall that first year as if it were yesterday, sitting around a table with a dozen dedicated volunteers, cutting out paper swans to glue on popsicle sticks with little feather boas—truly one of my favorite professional memories.

It's hard to believe that since then, we've flown Mary Poppins across the sky, constructed Snoopy's doghouse in Fenway Park's right field, and created a grand ball courtesy of Belle and her Beast, with massive candlesticks everywhere (inspired by Lumière, of course). We've visited Winnie the Pooh's Hundred Acre Wood, with bears and honey bottles and the whole space bathed in stunning, honey-colored light. We've had dinner on Treasure Island, under great sails suspended from the ceiling as if we were on an enormous pirate ship. Each time, we have evoked the spirit of a book, transporting our guests on an emotional journey to a magical place. It's an amazing challenge for us to strip off our inhibitions and approach an event the way a child might: nothing is too fantastical, and anything is possible.

What I like so much about the Storybook Ball is that it is different. It is not just another charity dinner in another hotel ballroom. Don't get me wrong, those can be wonderful and important, and you can make them beautiful. But a truly unique event can help a really great organization raise the money it needs to do its important work. These Storybook Balls have genuinely made a difference for sick kids for two decades. I love that we can do that.

PREVIOUS PAGE: Guests entered the Winnie the Pooh–themed Storybook Ball fundraiser for MassGeneral Hospital for Children through a hallway lined with bottles of honey. OPPOSITE: Laser-cut silhouettes of Christopher Robin and friends made of balsa wood adorned the tables.

WINNIE-THE-POOH

The Storybook parties are built around books, but they're not tacky theme parties. Each event needs to communicate the feeling of a classic book, but with the elegance and sophistication appropriate for our audience.

When we did *Winnie-the-Pooh*, for example, we thought about the thing that Pooh yearns for. Naturally, it's honey. So we had fun with that and let honey guide the design. We built a giant beehive that separated the cocktail area from the dining area, and we filled it with row upon row of those iconic little bear-shaped bottles of honey. We always love a chance to use massive amounts of one thing; the multiplicity effect creates magnificence. We just kept layering, and every other table had a honey-colored Plexiglas tabletop to give the room an even more honey-infused feel. And then, of course, in order to travel to the Hundred Acre Wood, we introduced branches to the design. Through state-of-the-art projections, we were able to amplify the impact of the table centerpieces, ensconcing the guests in Christopher Robin's magical world.

Small, simple, inexpensive things can make for big design ideas—and one great party. The honey bears are in every supermarket, and tree branches are everywhere. Putting on a beautiful, elegant, original party is, more than anything else, about creativity. Don't get me wrong: having a big budget is great. But there are all sorts of things you can do, and do well, if you really think creatively about the story you're telling.

Centerpieces made of pear branches, gloriosa lilies, dahlias, and oncidium orchids paired with video projections put guests inside the Hundred Acre Wood.

168

TOP AND BOTTOM LEFT: The honey theme included a giant beehive and pots of "hunny" on the cocktail tables. OPPOSITE: Hundreds of plastic honey bears combined to make a big impact—and cast a honey-colored glow on the room.

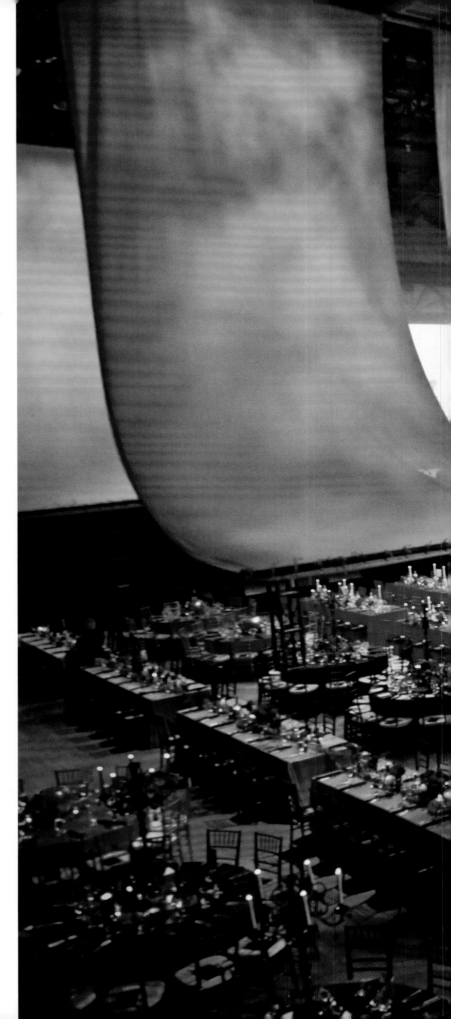

TREASURE ISLAND

When we think of *Treasure Island*, we think of all the classic pirate elements: big ships, stolen bounty, gold coins, hanging ropes, barrels filled with rum. Luckily, the enormous armory that hosts many of our Storybook Balls gave us the room to think big.

We thought about creating a replica of a sailing ship, on which we'd serve dinner. But it felt too obvious, and what's the fun in that? Instead, we opted for the essence of a large ship by creating towering masts and rigging big pieces of sailcloth that billowed over the dining tables. The sails celebrated the military history of the space while also making the dining room feel more intimate. Once guests took their seats, the unusual experience and dynamic surroundings fostered many interesting conversations.

We always like to find new and unexpected ways for people to experience an event venue, especially one they've visited before. We often move the entrance to a gala to have guests come in through the back door instead of the front. For this party, we had guests walk down a dark alleyway as a prelude to their big entrance. The alley became a great opportunity to begin the story of *Treasure Island*, complete with dozens of rum barrels, hundreds of yards of ship rope, and a salty pirate. The guests had visited this hall a dozen times before, but this pirate's alley made it feel like they were there for the first time.

Billowing sails turned the cavernous former armory into a pirate ship.

OPPOSITE, CLOCKWISE FROM TOP LEFT: We used barrels and fraying ship ropes to enhance the pirate theme. Dinner was served under the sails we installed. Dark sunflowers paired with deep-hued calla lilies and burgundy tropical leaves set an ominous tone. A pirate statue fit the theme. RIGHT: Amber candlesticks and golden treasure suggested a pirate's booty.

HOUSE PARTY

Almost fifteen years ago, we were asked to create a gala fundraising event for Boys & Girls Clubs of Boston, an amazing organization that provides a safe haven filled with hope and opportunity for the young people who need it most. Our marching orders were to make the event stand out, make it celebratory, and reinforce the great work the clubs were doing by telling their story in a simple way. Above all, we needed to entice new and existing benefactors alike to turn out for what the organizers hoped would become an annual gathering.

We started with the venue search. Our goal was to provide an elevated guest experience while highlighting those whom the Boys & Girls Clubs serve. We realized that the values, support, and connections that the clubs work hard to promote are ultimately built and strengthened most fully at home. So where better to beautifully highlight these ideals than at home? Thus, together with a very dedicated volunteer committee, House Party was born. And it has become the ultimate house party: an annual fundraising gala hosted each year by a different Boys & Girls Clubs benefactor in the backyard of their beautiful home.

When you open up your home to gather your friends and family, it is a very special gesture. Here, it also resonates perfectly with the organization we're supporting, which builds and runs clubhouses that provide a home away from home for kids who need places to study and play. Each year, we host more than five hundred people at the House Party, and since its inception, the gala has raised tens of millions of dollars.

Every nonprofit benefits from an original idea that simply and effectively tells the story of the work it does. The House Party does that for the Boys & Girls Clubs. But we also want to be sure that the guests' focus is ultimately on the group's mission, not just on the gorgeous home they're visiting. That's why we integrate photos of the clubs' kids in all of our designs and sometimes even place those pictures in the windows of the home. We want the faces and stories of these kids to be a big part of the evening's narrative and the clubs' mission to be the first and last thing guests think about.

The real focus of a House Party is the kids whose lives are changed. By placing photos of the kids in the house's front windows, we made sure they were the first thing guests saw as they arrived and the last thing they remembered as they left.

LEFT: One thousand salmon-colored peonies on the tables represented 1,000 kids who benefit from the clubhouses.
OPPOSITE AND FOLLOWING PAGES: The faces of the kids who benefit from the money raised reminded guests why they contribute.

HAPPY CAMPERS

Show character. Be courageous. Build community. These are a few of the principles Camp Harbor View teaches more than nine hundred kids from underserved Boston neighborhoods each summer during its two monthlong camp sessions on Long Island in Boston Harbor. Ferried across the harbor every day to and from camp, campers are transported into a world ruled by the organization's first and most important tenet: Have fun! Through a carefully crafted program grounded in the magic of summer camp—complete with boating, arts, athletics, music, and swimming—kids are exposed to learning and leadership opportunities that form a road map for healthy growth and lasting connections.

The founder of the camp came to us more than a decade ago with the idea to create an event that would raise money and remind donors how the wonders of summer camp can liberate the potential of young people. The kids he wanted to bring to camp had never conceived of an opportunity like this; many, despite living a stone's throw from the ocean, had never even left their neighborhoods. As we contemplated a celebration of everything that happens at camp, we introduced the Beach Ball.

We transform the same sprawling warehouse near Boston's waterfront for each ball, challenging ourselves to come up with new and exciting takes on summer camp and the beach every year. We never want it to feel like a theme party—our goal is to get to the essence of the camp experience. This is also a big event in a big space, so outsize impressions are key to ensuring its success. In cavernous spaces, we always begin with the largest elements, and the ceiling is a great place to start. When you are in a room with a thousand people having dinner, what do you see? Look up. The ceiling is a blank canvas for us to take a multitude of small things and make one very big statement using hundreds of yards of string lights or thousands of colored pennants that evoke a classic camp anywhere in the Northeast.

Camp Harbor View is a place where everyone is energized and smiling. We channel that amazing energy into event designs that lead donors old and new on the camp journey time and time again.

Yellow, blue, and green are the colors of summer—sun, water, and grass. More than six dozen beach umbrellas hung from the ceiling evoked a joyful expression of the summer camp.

THE ESSENCE
OF SUMMER

Our philosophy is always that a party should highlight the thing being celebrated, not attempt to replicate it. For the Beach Ball, we were not looking for the full summer-camp experience. No hot dogs or bug juice here! Instead, we used striking design elements that get at the essence of the beach, like two hundred blue-and-white beach umbrellas hung upside down from the ceiling. An individual beach umbrella would feel like a theme party, but hundreds of them become a beautiful artistic statement. We covered the whole floor with bright green carpeting to evoke the ball fields at camp.

Everything was yellow, blue, and green, the colors of summer: sun, water, and grass. Some tables had blue-and-white gingham cloths, while others were patterned with big green leaves. But all of the table centerpieces were bright yellow sunflowers, which gave a giant impression as you looked across the room.

TOP LEFT: The "Have a Voice" microphone sitting atop the menu was actually a clever pledge card. BOTTOM LEFT: Oversize buffalo-check linens, woven dinner chargers, and sunflowers dressed each dinner table. OPPOSITE: Tall glass vessels were filled with single sunflowers and hosta leaves to offset the height of the big room.

REBRANDING SUMMER

A new year presented another chance to capture the essence of summer. But this time, there was an added wrinkle: Camp Harbor View had just rebranded, and their signature color was now orange. They wanted everyone to really feel that new brand, so it was our chance to take on summer from a different direction, all while showing off the camp's fresh look. All of the flowers were orange, the tablecloths had orange and white stripes, and there were orange napkins and orange cushions on the chairs.

We also took advantage of the big space by mounting a huge wall of video screens. We shot videos of the ferry ride to camp, looking back at Boston, of activities at camp, and of camp-style signage. The kids aren't just hanging out at Camp Harbor View; they're also learning and growing. We wanted to make sure donors knew there was real substance to their experience.

Pennants are classic decorations that suggested a cookout or field day. They were also a creative way to give visual interest to the bare ceiling of this industrial space.

186

LEFT: Orange calla lilies and liriope grasses created height and movement, while striped linens suggested saltwater taffy and the beach.
OPPOSITE: The orange room highlighted the camp's new brand color.

PART III

Celebrating the White House

Designing parties for the White House is a special opportunity. You want each event to be unique, but you're constantly reminded of where you are. The house is both filled with American history and part of it. We knew that hundreds of legendary parties and celebrations had come before us. Striking the right mix of respect and originality was always an exciting challenge.

I helped Michelle Obama design seven state dinners and fifteen other celebrations during her husband's administration. Mrs. Obama's vision aligned beautifully with our guiding principles; she always wanted to tell the story of the country, people, or program we were honoring. She—and we— also wanted each event to be unlike any other, because visiting the White House is a once-in-a-lifetime experience. But best was that Mrs. Obama loved color. We could make our celebrations stand out when we had all the colors of the rainbow at our disposal.

STATE DINNERS

The first state dinner I designed with Mrs. Obama was in honor of Hu Jintao, president of China, in 2011. I've built my business on relationships, and I suspect Hillary Clinton gave me a good recommendation after I planned and executed her daughter Chelsea's wedding weekend in the summer of 2010.

As the planning started, I received a one-page briefing from the White House with a list of President Hu's known likes and dislikes. I would get one of these before each state dinner, listing color preferences, food likes or dislikes, and preferred entertainers. (Beyoncé was listed as a top choice just about every time.) But that was about it for direction. So I went out and found a book called *Chinese Symbolism and Art Motifs*, and that became my bible. I carried it with me to meetings. I presented fabric designs and color choices—and turned oranges into centerpieces!—because of what I learned from that book.

That plan carried through to all the other state dinners I designed; I'd always investigate symbolism and cultural touchstones for the honored country. Mrs. Obama and her staff knew they could count on me to present a story that had depth and meaning. I wanted each one to be unlike anything that had been in the house before, but at the same time I wanted to honor all of the house's gorgeous detailing. For one, I built frames around the twelve-foot-tall gilded wall mirrors in the East Room, so that we could surround them with flowers and make them look different than they ever had.

Mrs. Obama was always warm and friendly, determined and focused. I learned quickly that the best way to present ideas to her was for me to be clear, concise, and as visual as possible. For each event we planned, we'd present at least three concepts, shown to the First Lady and her team in binders that included floor plans, design elements, sample photos, and fabric swatches. The more samples I could show Mrs. Obama, the better. She wanted to see what we were thinking and comprehend the story we wanted to tell on her behalf. She understood the importance of design and diplomacy, and she was comfortable making bold choices.

PREVIOUS PAGE: On the morning of June 26, 2015, the Supreme Court issued its decision in *Obergefell v. Hodges*, legalizing same-sex marriage across the country. That night, we lit the north facade of the White House with a rainbow. OPPOSITE: Teal velvet tablecloths contrasted with centerpieces of pink peonies and fuchsia orchids.

CHERRY BLOSSOMS
FOR JAPAN

A state visit is a celebration of America's relationship with another country, and the state honors that country and its leader. When I was planning the dinner in honor of Shinzo Abe, the prime minister of Japan, I realized that there's a very obvious symbol of our friendship with his country just a few blocks away from the White House: the 3,020 cherry trees Tokyo's mayor gave to the United States in 1912.

The cherry blossoms peaked in early April that year, and the dinner wasn't until the end of that month, so I ordered hundreds and hundreds of blossoming cherry branches from a greenhouse and filled the main hallway on the State Floor with them. I had the pleasure of standing in the doorway when Mrs. Abe walked through with Mrs. Obama on the afternoon of the reception, and I watched her enter the hall and gasp. She'd never seen so many cherry blossoms in one place indoors. That's exactly the kind of reaction we were hoping for with this memorable and abundant symbol of the warm relations between our two countries.

For this dinner we used the Obama china, which features a bright teal stripe inside a gold rim. Mrs. Obama calls the color Kailua Blue, inspired by the waters off her husband's home state. We paired the china with teal velvet tablecloths. It's another example of Mrs. Obama's enthusiasm for bold colors and bold choices.

Patterned light projected on the ceiling echoed the massed cherry-blossom branches lining the Cross Hall.

194

THIS PAGE AND OPPOSITE:
Spring flowers, including
cherry branches, peonies,
orchids, roses, lilacs,
and vine and fern accents,
dressed the State Floor
of the White House.

LEFT, CLOCKWISE FROM TOP LEFT: We created pavés of vibrant roses and peonies in frames surrounding antique mirrors. We also used the flowers in a backdrop to give the East Room a punch of color. Crystal curtains hung in the windows and bounced light around the room. Red chopsticks complemented the floral centerpieces. OPPOSITE: Teal tablecloths offset the pink flowers. FOLLOWING PAGES: Martha and George Washington watched over the glowing pink room.

AN ENGLISH GARDEN FOR THE UNITED KINGDOM

For this dinner in honor of David Cameron, then the British prime minister, we were outside and under a tent. The State Dining Room can fit up to 236 dinner guests; anything bigger than that, and you need to move outside.

To tell the story of the great friendship between our two countries, I wanted to turn the South Lawn, that classic American backyard, into an English garden. We created floating flower boxes that divided the big tent into four unique areas—we thought of those florals as hedgerows. They made the evening garden-like, but they also helped make the big tented space feel intimate and the event more like a family affair. We also used three different table designs, each with different linens, different candles, and different floral centerpieces, to create one large, lively canvas, as guests looked across the space.

The real design signature was purple everywhere, with a splash of chartreuse. The purple was for Mrs. Obama; it's one of her favorite colors. She loves the Lincoln china, for example, because it has a dramatic purple rim. Unfortunately, the curators didn't let us use the historic White House china for events—just the sets from recent presidents. When the First Lady was selecting the Obama china, she learned that modern purple dyes don't work well on fine china. That's why she picked that vibrant blue instead.

Outside the tent, visible to all the guests, was a mighty Japanese maple, bare because it was wintertime. So we covered it with thousands of silk butterflies (in purple and chartreuse, of course), to represent endurance, change, and hope, qualities expressed in the close U.S.-British friendship.

Hedgerows enhanced the garden feeling of the dinner while also helping to break the vast tented dining room into more intimate spaces.

Purple roses in perfect rows, resting on mirrored footing and partnered with purple lilacs in a glass vase, complemented the purple and silver–satin linens. There was also a soft green touch in the hemstitched napkins.

OPPOSITE: Gathered sweet peas and vibrant green hydrangeas formed our English garden centerpieces. RIGHT: We also used vanda orchids and faux butterfly accents.

LOOKING TO THE FUTURE WITH GERMANY

The state dinner in honor of Angela Merkel, the chancellor of Germany, was one of my favorites. We weren't just outside; we were in the Rose Garden in spring. That meant no tent; just a beautiful Washington sky overhead.

In honor of our close relationship with Germany and our two countries' focus on the future, we gave this dinner a very modern, clean look. Everything was white—white tables, white chairs, white linens, even white carpet on the wood floor we built over the grass. The flowers were tightly structured, angular, and architectural. Against the natural backdrop of the Rose Garden, in the twilight once evening fell, it looked stunning.

We woke up that morning to a beautiful day, but there was just one problem: the National Weather Service was predicting a 20 percent chance of rain. We had a call in the morning about whether to move ahead with the Social Office, the house staff, and a few dozen other officials, including the National Weather Service. I was listening quietly, on mute. After a robust discussion, the person from the weather service gave his report and then asked if I was on the call. "Mr. Rafanelli must have experience with this," he said. I did. "It's like investing," I told the group. "If you've got an 80 percent chance of success, you go for it." People started clicking off the call. Amazingly enough, I'd made the decision. Even better: it never rained.

TOP LEFT: We dressed the tables with crisp white linens and clean, simple florals of green viburnums and hydrangeas with yellow calla lilies. BOTTOM LEFT: The place settings were the Bush Presidential china. OPPOSITE: We used both long and round tables arranged on a white and gray–carpeted floor built over the Rose Garden.

OLD-WORLD ELEGANCE
FOR ITALY

The state dinner in honor of Matteo Renzi, then the prime minister of Italy, was the final state dinner of the Obama administration, just a few weeks before the 2016 election. This one was outside on the South Lawn under a big glass tent.

I saw that as a bonus, because I love the sense of surprise a tent can provide. Being outside is a different and unique experience, but I also want a tent to feel like part of the house. This was an exciting opportunity to re-create the feeling of the White House outdoors.

To celebrate Italy, I gave this dinner a classic, old-world feel. We used dozens of crystal chandeliers and elegant upholstered chairs. In contrast to the bold, vibrant colors of our other dinners, we kept the palette to muted tones inspired by the frescoes of the Italian Renaissance. We also created arrangements of garden roses, spray roses, ranunculuses, nerines, sedums, euphorbias, hydrangeas, and seasonal foliage, all in pale tones that harmonized with the simple cream-colored linens.

This dinner had a special poignancy, and not just because it was President Obama's last one. I'm Italian-American. So is Gwen Stefani, who performed that night. It was always an honor to design parties at the White House, but on this night I was especially proud to be there.

Custom upholstered dining chairs created a residential feel in the tented dining room. We placed more than four dozen crystal-topped candelabras on the tables.

OPPOSITE: Mirrored surfaces, cement chargers, and gold accents created unexpected juxtapositions on the tabletops. RIGHT: The flowers were spray and garden roses, passion vines, nerines, and astilbes, all in soft pastel tones.

We created a grand entryway
to the tent with a path across the
South Lawn, lit by antiqued
glass hurricanes and lined with
manicured shrubbery.

MOVEABLE FEASTS

Mrs. Obama's signature project as First Lady was the "Let's Move!" campaign, her effort to get kids to exercise and eat well. Each year, she'd run the Healthy Lunchtime Challenge, which invited kids to create original recipes for a healthy, affordable, and tasty lunch and then submit them to the competition. The fifty-six winning kids—one from each state and territory—were then invited to the White House for what we called the Kids' State Dinner (which was really a lunch). Mrs. Obama's staff always said those were her favorite events at the White House.

We worked on all five Kids' State Dinners, and we followed the same principles we always did in the White House: make each dinner look new and different while respecting the integrity of the house. But we were also allowed to be more playful than usual. Every year we created unique towering centerpieces made out of fresh vegetables. On the fifth year, the tagline was "Gimme Five," and we printed that hashtag on napkin rings that doubled as bracelets for the kids. We also created a big stage backdrop made out of yellow peppers and red carnations in the shape of a big hand—gimme five!

It was so much fun watching the kids enter these state dinners and seeing the awestruck looks on their faces. It's actually what I think everyone feels every time they come into the White House, but unlike grown-ups, the kids don't try to hide it.

Fun, healthy vegetable topiaries, made of cherry tomatoes, brussels sprouts, and radishes, adorned the tables. The oversized gingham pattern on the linens provided the perfect scale and splash of color for the large space.

OPPOSITE: Guests were greeted by a towering arrangement of kale, corn on the cob, eggplants, pomegranates, peppers, and apples. All of the perishable items were donated to a food pantry after the event. RIGHT, CLOCKWISE FROM TOP: The First Lady's place card. Rubber bracelets served as napkin rings. Sweatbands were party favors—and inspiration to get the kids moving.

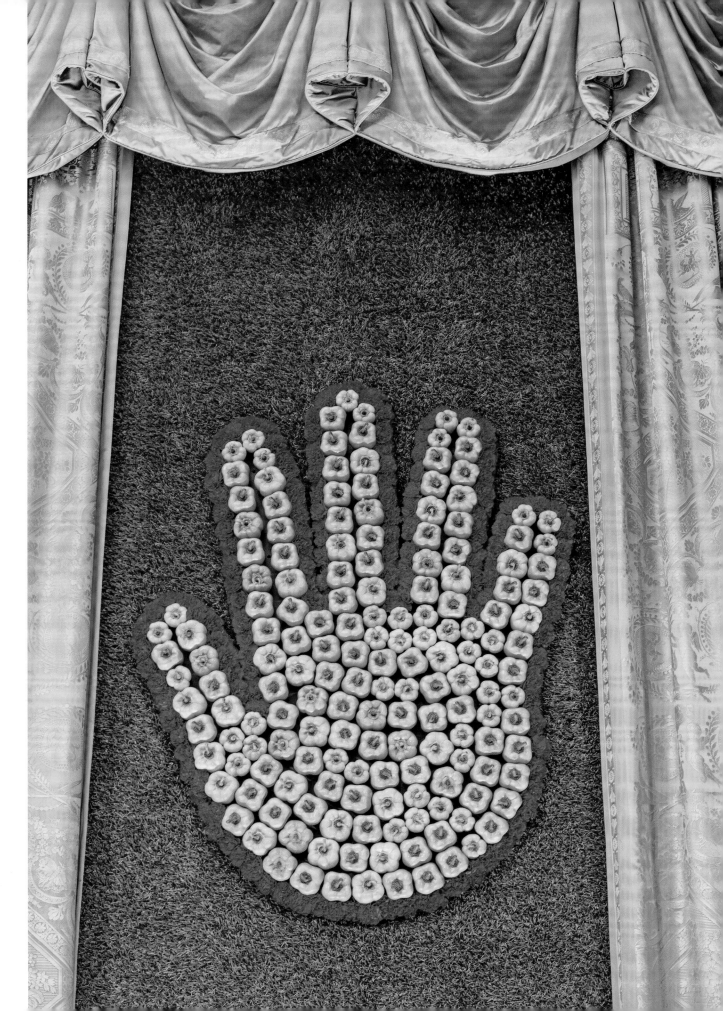

OPPOSITE: Big masses of a single item always create a fun, contemporary splash of color. THIS PAGE: A bell-pepper and carnation hand on a field of turf served as a backdrop and illustrated the First Lady's theme of "Gimme Five!"

CHRISTMAS IN THE WHITE HOUSE

Christmas at the White House is simply all-American: a grand old house filled with lights and decorations. But there was nothing simple about it. We would begin installing decorations on the night of Thanksgiving, working with one hundred volunteers from around the United States. Fifty-six trees, more than a hundred wreaths, and hundreds of yards of green garland were spread out over the main house, the private residence, and the West Wing.

I wanted each year to have a symbol—an iconic image. One year, we went to Washington, D.C., public schools and asked kids to make those folded-up paper snowflakes. They wrote their holiday wishes on them. We hung 3,000 of those snowflakes in the East Colonnade overlooking the First Lady's garden. The students' snowflakes were mixed with fifty-six 18-inch Plexiglas snowflakes. It wasn't anything fancy, with everything just hanging from some chicken wire we placed along the ceiling. But massed together, the look was totally cool and took great advantage of the high ceilings and big volume of that hall.

Another year, we filled the State Dining Room with decorations for the kids who would visit, many of them children of active-duty service members. There were enormous trees, trees made from candy, and gifts and presents all around. I loved the image of the nutcrackers and a giant teddy bear sitting in front of the fireplace, with Abraham Lincoln looking down from a portrait above the mantelpiece. It looked exactly as Christmas at the White House should.

Fifty-six snowmen and fifty-six snowflakes symbolized America's fifty-six states and territories. The custom jewelbox snowflakes were accompanied by more than 3,000 hand-cut paper snowflakes made by local schoolchildren.

OPPOSITE: The 2016 White House holiday theme was "The Gift of the Season," and how better to arrive for a party than by walking through a giant (and very Instagrammable) gift? RIGHT: The First Lady in front of one of the four trees we decorated for the East Room.

OPPOSITE, CLOCKWISE FROM TOP LEFT: We used ornaments from previous White House holiday celebrations to create a giant pavé surrounding a column. A 200-foot garland attached to a ramp at the east entrance was adorned with more recycled multicolored ornaments. We hung pine garlands wrapped in thousands of white lights and double wrapped with a red garland made of ruby-red glass ornaments on each mirror in the East Room. For the Green Room, a more classic presentation. RIGHT: The People's Tree, in the Blue Room, was decorated with stripes of red, white, and blue, with a garland of solid-gold stars. The white ribbon was calligraphed with messages to service members from their families.

You can create fun juxtapositions in the White House, like surrounding a portrait of Abraham Lincoln with topiary trees made of candy canes and gumballs, evergreens decorated with hundreds of toys, and nutcrackers standing sentry. FOLLOWING PAGES: More White House holiday decorations, including the first-ever glazed-but-unfrosted gingerbread White House, designed by White House pastry chef Susie Morrison, and a Lego White House.

Merry Christmas Andy. Another Christmas apart, but you are in our thoughts and in our hearts. Love to you in South Korea. Mom and Dad.

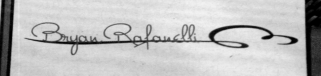

Bryan Rafanelli

Lobster-Watermelon-Tomato

Lobster, Heirloom Tomatoes, Melon Balls, Pea & Corn Shoots,
Green Curry and Pickled Ginger Vinaigrette

Summer BBQ Trio

LEFT: Kraft-paper menu cards on rattan chargers, with (of course) Starbucks-accented water glasses. OPPOSITE: Party details represented all things me, including plaids, Provincetown, neckties, and my beloved golden retriever, Henry Rafanelli.

PART V

Rafanelli's Rules

During my twenty years in this business, I've found myself returning to a handful of principles again and again. Some of them are party classics, and some are unique to the way I like to make a celebration special. But they're all in service of the same essential goal: the key to a great party is making your celebration memorable and all about you. Whether it's a wedding, an anniversary, a charity gala, or even a state dinner, your party should be unforgettable and unlike anything your guests have seen before. You want to surprise your guests, wow them, and provide them with moments of intimacy, excitement, and wonder. These rules help us create perfect parties, and they hold true regardless of occasion, location, or budget. They allow you to create a celebration that's perfectly, uniquely, magnificently yours.

THINK BIG

S ize makes a statement. Oversize design elements are eye-catching, exciting, and full of energy. And they often display a sense of fun and whimsy; they get a laugh. They're impossible to forget.

For the holidays at the Obama White House, we (along with one hundred volunteers) created models of the First Dogs, Bo and Sunny, that were eight and six feet tall, respectively, and made out of more than 30,000 black and white balls of yarn. The kids who came to holiday parties were crazy for them—and the adults even more so.

Sometimes we take one component of a celebration and blow it way out of scale. For a wedding after-party, we placed the DJ booth at the top of a two-story boldly patterned wall. The wall separated dinner from dancing, and it also made clear that the music experience at this party would be giant.

Creating shifts in perspective is another way to use scale. Doing that can even turn the ballroom itself into a visual statement, one of my favorite shifts. We'll often design a small entryway leading into the main event. That lets us build a great sense of arrival as the guests move from an intimate space into the expansive main room. It is an extraordinary moment when guests get that first glimpse of the ballroom as they emerge from a tunnel of greenery, step through a twelve-foot-wide floral wall, and then encounter a riot of color. It announces that something very special is about to happen.

PREVIOUS PAGE: A bride and groom are announced, with hundreds of Mylar ballons setting the backdrop. LEFT: Oversize versions of Bo and Sunny Obama, made from thousands of spools of yarn. OPPOSITE: A forty-foot-wide and sixteen-foot-tall colorful striped DJ booth set the tone for an amazing after-party.

PART IV

The Guest of Honor

Don't tell anyone, but when I turned fifty, I had a big birthday party.

I was loving my life, my career, my business. I wanted to bring together everyone I knew and loved and thank them all for helping me get to where I was.

It was a killer party.

But the best part was that I didn't plan or design it. Well, I was a little bit involved. I picked the date. I chose the guest list—my family, my friends, all the longtime clients who've become friends, and my great staff. And I picked the venue, the big, beautiful old town hall in one of my favorite places in the world: Provincetown, Massachusetts. But then my amazing partner and my creative team did everything else for me. As I always tell clients considering a surprise party: No one likes a true surprise, but everyone loves not to have to plan his or her own party.

They came up with a design that truly told my story. I love red, white, and blue—I even collect old flags—so that was the color scheme, with a pop of bright green. I have a few hundred gingham shirts in my closet, so they went crazy with all different sizes of checks and plaids. (Good thing I decided to wear a simple gray suit!) I always have a giant cup of Starbucks coffee with me, so every water glass on the tables got a Starbucks sleeve. I worshipped my golden retriever, Henry, so they created a silhouette of him and found several places to showcase his handsome face. And then, because I always like things to be both a little bit old-fashioned and a little bit over-the-top, they hired a twenty-five-piece orchestra, all in white dinner jackets.

Everyone important to me was in that room: the clients who got me started; the clients who helped me grow; my mother and brothers and sisters and nieces and nephews; my amazing team; even some of my talented suppliers—because they're part of how I can do what I do.

It was definitely me, as every celebration you throw should be about you. If you choose the right time, the right place, and the right people for your party, and let good friends and family do the rest, you'll have the time of your life. I know I did.

I was big into plaid at the time, so my team's design tribute to me made extensive use of gingham and other plaids. FOLLOWING PAGES: The Provincetown Town Hall's auditorium was decked out in red, white, and blue for the celebration.

DON'T EXPECT THE
UNEXPECTED—CREATE IT

We all want our parties to be unforgettable. And one way to do that is to change your guests' perspective.

There are some really simple ways to do that. If the standard arrangement at an elegant hotel ballroom puts the band on the east wall of the room and the bar on the west side, we'll flip it. If every gala has guests entering the museum lobby up the grand staircase, we'll try building a path to an alternate entryway.

We designed one party in a client's backyard under a classic white tent. When guests entered the tent, they found paneled black-lacquered walls and a black ceiling with mirrored details. LED screens were embedded into the paneled walls. It felt like a sophisticated nightclub, which no one was expecting in an outdoor tent.

For one of our annual parties for a children's hospital, we were tasked with bringing to life the story of *101 Dalmatians*. Because guests knew the theme before they arrived, they expected to find a black-and-white color scheme, perhaps with some diamonds or fur accents. Instead, they entered a quintessential British pub, circa 1956. Rather than going with the expected design, we instead transported our guests back to the time the story was set in. Even more delightful, a forty-foot-long wall behind the bar was covered in formal portraits not of ancestors but of dogs in all breeds, shapes, and sizes. The guests had a blast picking out their own dog ancestors!

Surprising guests is all about upending their expectations. It's what they'll remember.

A sexy supper club with a black-and-mirrored ceiling
was totally unexpected inside a backyard tent.

SHOULDERS AND ABOVE

My team knows well a mantra I use when designing an event: Shoulders and above. When you look across a cocktail party filled with guests, what do you see? The things above shoulder level. This view will be guests' first and last impressions of a party.

At a dinner, the guests' focus will be on the tabletop: fine china, crystal glasses, and elegant silverware, as well as linens, floral centerpieces, and flickering candlelight. That landscape is critical. But for an even more successful party, you need a design element that is a perfect complement to the meticulous table design, one which guests will see looking across the room.

A beautiful, eye-catching installation hanging from the ceiling—whether it's one large element or a series of smaller ones—is what guests will see when the party is in full swing and what they'll likely talk about afterward. For a summertime Hamptons wedding, we floated hundreds of white lanterns on airplane wire over the cocktails area to not only create a ceiling but also define the walls—in the middle of an open-air field. It was an elegant design element and a conversation piece throughout the party.

Whether the party is cocktails, a buffet dinner, or a formal seated affair, an eye-catching element above the shoulders can be one of the most impactful investments you will make.

LEFT: There's power in repeated patterns, like the high-gloss materiality of a four-tiered silver-and-gold mirrored chandelier.
OPPOSITE: Hundreds of organic white voile fabric panels adorned a ceiling.

BEAUTY IN NUMBERS

We've established that I like big, bold statements. And one of my favorite ways to make them is with a small item. Correction: a *lot* of small items. Guests are surprised and delighted when they see that the big visual signature in a room is actually composed of many, many things.

Arrange three hundred small votive candles across a patio to create a beautiful, sculptural shape. Pick up cast-off flowers from your local florist and then use those petals to create a walkway, or just strew them throughout your party. If you think about it, you'll start to realize that any party generates plenty of inventory that can be transformed into design elements. Hundreds of wine bottles lined up along a wall turn a bar into a statement. Crystal glasses hanging from the ceiling look luxe and eye-catching when they're suspended by the thousands.

I especially love when we make these bold statements with humble, everyday objects. During our holiday-season work at the White House, we discovered boxes upon boxes of small decorations that had sat unused for years, such as plastic and glass balls, tree lights in many colors, and pine cones. We turned them into fresh and new decorations by displaying them en masse, as garlands of plastic balls draped from doorways, wreaths shaped from strings of lights, and pine cone topiaries.

A little imagination—plus a lot of small items—goes a long way.

LEFT: Three thousand red, purple, and hot pink satin gift ribbons hung in the East Colonnade of the White House.
OPPOSITE: Nearly 2,000 red wine glasses were suspended over a mirrored bar, with 1,000 wine bottles as decoration.

SOMETHING FROM NOTHING

Pulling off all these great tricks—building oversize, striking design elements that amaze and fascinate your guests—doesn't always require the finest and most elegant materials. In fact, you can very often create gorgeous, luxurious features from some of the simplest, most commonplace elements.

My best inspiration often comes from the most mundane places. A visit to a corner drugstore while ruminating on ideas for White House holiday decor gave me the idea to create gorgeously patterned pavé pillars, all made out of thousands of small gift ribbons. Guests had to get within a few inches of the installations to figure out what they were looking at. We used No. 2 pencils to make topiaries to celebrate the First Lady's educational initiative for girls. And for a gala hosted by a charity that builds desks for schoolchildren in Africa, we built a backdrop from discarded packing crates from a home-supply store.

When we designed Mrs. Obama's Kids' State Dinners, we often created centerpieces and other design features out of fruits and vegetables. We've hung beach umbrellas from ceilings, built a chandelier from thousands of pieces of confetti, and formed centerpieces from high-top sneakers. Even after so many years in this business, I still get such joy when I come up with a deceptively easy design idea and conjure something beautiful from something simple. That's creativity at its essence; it's accessible to everyone and the key to a memorable event.

LEFT: Ten thousand drugstore gift bows covered a column in the East Wing of the White House. OPPOSITE: The bows were inexpensive, but from a distance they appeared deeply luxurious.

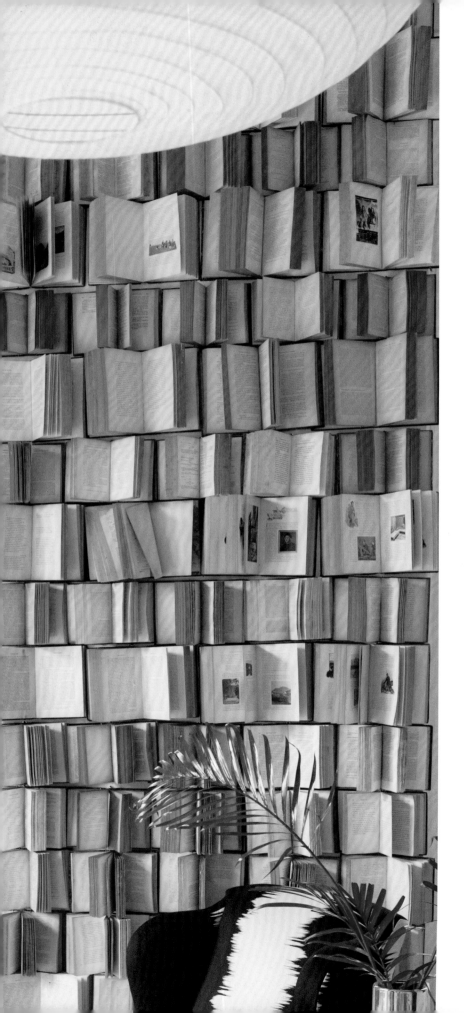

PLAIN AND SIMPLE

What I've come to realize in my years of designing celebrations is that the real trick is not to overthink things. We obsess over logistics and execution, of course. But for the big ideas, the best strategy is to keep things simple.

If you're throwing a housewarming party, tell a story about moving, with decorations made from cardboard boxes and Bubble Wrap. If you're designing a book signing, decorate with books. I once designed a store opening where we made sure that every decoration we used was something that you could open up. This kind of common-sense simplicity is what will resonate with your guests and make them remember the story you're telling.

I often say that the key to any design is distilling the story to its essence. If I'm paying tribute to a city, to a great cause, or to a charismatic couple, I never want to design a theme party that dutifully mimics everything about its subject. What I want to do is get down to those key attributes, then elegantly reflect those qualities back in the design.

LEFT: A backdrop made from more than 250 vintage books.
OPPOSITE: For a moving-themed party, we lined the room in hundreds of moving boxes and used furniture upholstered in Bubble Wrap.

TELL A STORY

Ultimately, all of these rules are designed to help tell a great story. At its essence, a party is a shared experience for you and your guests. You've taken them on a journey that they will remember forever. And when you find a way to do that, to tell your story, you will have created a great party.

If the story is that you're providing needy schoolkids with free eye exams and eyewear, run with the details of that story: decorate with eyes, frames, and beautiful illustrations of people wearing eyeglasses. If you're celebrating in a vineyard, create centerpieces out of grapes instead of flowers and use grape leaves to adorn your dinner napkins.

Or take inspiration from your own personality and your own brand. Mrs. Obama was focused on healthy eating, so for her Kids' State Dinners we took nature's bounty and made that our decor. If you're from Baltimore, throw a crab boil, complete with picnic linens and bibs. If you're planning an anniversary party to celebrate a sixty-year love affair, reminisce about those old times with waiters in white tie, an orchestra, and classic cocktails like martinis and Manhattans.

There is no singular formula for success, other than to start with the story. Find its beginning, its middle, and its end. Let guests experience it through all their senses—with music, flowers, and food all perfectly suited to the night. That story is what will turn an average party into a great party, one your guests will never forget.

LEFT: For a UNICEF gala, we built a wall stocked with slips of writing paper representing the 6,000 lives the organization saves every day.
OPPOSITE: A L'Objet plate decorated with an eye on custom-illustrated table linens with more eye designs for KREWE Foundation, which provides eye exams and eyewear to New Orleans high-school students.

ACKNOWLEDGMENTS

I am indebted to many people for my business, my career, this book, and my life. Thank you to:

THE FRIENDS: You are there for me whenever I need you, and I appreciate all the great advice and belief in me as a person. You have made my life so rich and meaningful. Mary Hull, Frederic Boudet, Leo Fifis, Bobby Kelley, Donna Montgomery, Dan Mullin, and Lauren Pellegrino.

THE GAME CHANGERS: With a world of choices available to you, you took a chance on me, and you changed the trajectory of my work and my life forever. I am eternally grateful. Roberta and Stephen Weiner, Barbara Jordan, Elaine and Gerry Schuster, Jack Connors, and Charlotte Vena.

MY "FIRST" FIRST FAMILY: Thank you for making me part of your family and a part of history. Bill and Hillary Clinton, Chelsea Clinton and Marc Mezvinsky, and Dorothy Rodham.

THE OBAMA WHITE HOUSE: Michelle Obama, thank you for welcoming me into the People's House, for your warmth, and for allowing me the opportunity to listen, interpret, and act on your creative vision. This great house is filled with extraordinary people who give themselves each and every day to our country. Thank you for letting me spend some time there and be a small part of history. Tina Chen, Jim Doherty, Laura Dowling, Dale Henley, Valerie Jarrett, Angela Reid, Joe Reinstein, Daniel Shanks, Jeff Tiller, Melissa Winters, and the hundreds of 2015 and 2016 White House holiday volunteers from around the United States.

THE SOCIALS: Jeremy Bernard, Deesha Dyer, and Julianna Smoot. It was a privilege to work with three truly extraordinary White House social secretaries, and with the U.S. Chief of Protocol, Capricia Penavic Marshall.

THE CLINTON TEAM: You make it all happen. Thank you for your loyalty, your kindness, and your friendship. Huma Abedin, Dennis Cheng, Hannah Richert, and Bari Lurie.

THE EARLY INVESTORS: Thank you for being early believers. Pat and Jon Baker, Ted and Joan Cutler, Randi and Joel Cutler, Peter Dominski, Lynne and Stu Elfland, William Evers, Deborah Farley, Sally Funk, Paul Grant, Patty and Brad Griffith, Mary Ellen Heinen and Len Kawell, Melissa and Andy Janfaza, Darlene and Jerry Jordan, Nina Jung, Michele and Howard Kessler, Myra and Robert Kraft, Beth Kurtin, Kay Martin, and Sharon McNally.

OUR COMMITTED CLIENTS AND FRIENDS: You have shaped my business and my person in countless ways. I am steadfastly grateful. Alli and Bill Achtmeyer, Judy and Dick Agee, Hannah and John Anderson, Kathryn Arce and Rebecca Grinnals, Lyndsay Magid and Josh Avenir, Susan Awes, Gary Bahre, Sandy and Bob Bahre, Mark Baranski, Amy and John Berylson, Jennifer and Jonathan Block, Marcy Blum, Marcia and Robin Brown, Tina Brown, Ed Byrnes, Lucy and Matt Damon, Margot and Jon Davis, Meredith DeWitt, Sandy and Paul Edgerley, Sister Janet Eisner, Anne Esposito, Debbie and Alan Ezekowitz, Joe Fallon, Christine Farris, Jesse Tyler Ferguson and Justin Mikita, Jerry Finegold, Anne Finucane, Phyllis and Paul Fireman, Gretchen and Ed Fish, Susan and Paul Flynn, Richard Friedman, Kathy Gasperine, Lucretia Gilbert, Jill Goldweitz, Adam Hagen, Linda and John Henry, Steve Huber, Arianna Huffington, Chris Hughes and Sean Eldridge, Jim Husson, Robert Isabell, Sinesia and Bill Karol, Elizabeth Berylson Katz and Rob Katz, Beth and Seth Klarman, Martha and Ron Kleinman, Brian Knez, Joshua Kraft, Sandy Kurson, Leonard Lauder, Jane Lavine, Lisa and Steve Lebovitz, Cindy and Richard Leibovitch, Joyce Linde, Dan Linn, Liz Lovett, Stacey and Larry Lucchino, Peter and Carolyn Lynch, Deborah and Herb Magid, Heather McDowell and Adam Levin, Michael Mazzaferro, Anne McNulty, Brynne McNulty and Julio Rojas Sarmiento, Steve Melvard, Connie Milstein, Betsy Nabel, Sandy and Joe O'Connor, Liz Page, Michelle Rago, Steve Rasnik, Patty and Charles Ribakoff, Erin and Paul Riley, Alison Rinderknecht, Sarah Sallee and David Rosengarten, Jaleh and Bruce Sallee, Alexandra Schuster and Alexander Sloane, Audrey and Mark Schuster, Heidi and Scott Schuster, Bingo Sears, Samantha Sherman, Barbara Silverstein, Peter Slavin, Gilda and Fred Slifka, Dana and Rob Smith, Barbara Spencer, Jillian Sullivan, Mike Taylor, Rita and Adam Weiner, Laura Wernick, Allison Williams and Ricky Van Veen, Jane and Brian Williams, and Ronny Zinner.

PARTNERS, FRIENDS, AND TALENT: I have been blessed to work with the most creative and talented suppliers in the world. The images on the pages of this book are a shining example of all that you have given to me and to so many grateful clients. You are the talent that makes each one of our parties unique and purposeful. I am eternally appreciative for the amazing ideas, long hours, creative thinking, and exceptional execution. David Adler, Heather Arak-Kanofsky and Susan Arak Turnock, Neal Balkowitsch, Collin Barnard, Ellen Bartlett, John Benke, Cheree Berry and Kristen Armstrong, Kym Bichon, Chris Burmester, Eric Chauvin, Olivier Cheng, Jon Cini, Sandi Chudnow, Maureen Curreri Collier, Fred Elting, Ruth Fischl, Julie Fox, Josh Friedman, Steve Frost, Todd Gerrish, Olivier Giugni, Bettina Hakko, JoAnn Harding, Ceci Johnson, Candan Kiramer, Denise Kirk, Mary Lampariello, Murray Lapidus, Karin Larson, Jeff Leatham, Doris Leonard, Lisa Luchetti, Veronica Martell, Dan Mathieu, Chris McMeen, Bentley Meeker, Joe Messina, Darcy Miller, Guy-Jeff Nelson, Benjamin Newbold, Dave O'Leary, Pablo Oliveira, Georgia Patton, John Pergantis, Jim Peters, Cindy Powers, Alexa Pulitzer, Ken Quigley, Julie Sabatino, Holly Safford, Elizabeth Slossberg, Nick Spanswick, Bill Taylor, Marco Tixe, Bob Traina, Christine Traulich, Jimmy Vali, Dini von Mueffling, Sylvia Weinstock, Simone Williamson, Keith Willis, Sarah Winward, Joel Wolke, Chris Zeig, and a special thank you to our invaluable floral partner, Ted Winston and Winston Flowers.

THE INCREDIBLE BOOK TEAM: This journey has been incredibly exciting and fulfilling—really, a dream come true. Thank you for believing in this book and for the countless hours of great ideas, creativity, and advice. David Kuhn, Andrew LaPrade, Alex Levy, Kate Mack, Jesse Oxfeld, and a special thank you to Emily Plourde. And Kathleen Jayes, Charles Miers, Steve Turner, Doug Turshen, and the entire Rizzoli team.

TEAM RAFANELLI: I have been lucky to work with the most creative, talented, smart, and amusing people on the planet. The events featured in this book and the hundreds executed over the past twenty-three years are the result of a giant collaboration. We did this together, through long hours, major challenges, miracles, and more. Thank you, thank you, thank you to Team Rafanelli. Taryn Antoniou, Hara Aoki-Saffer, Kaitlin Arcario, Adam Awes, Amanda Butler, Kaleigh Crowell, Alexandra DaRosa, Samuel Davis, Sarah Anne DiNardo, Torrey Hancock, Jacquelyn Johnson, Jane Miller, Michelle Mutter, Mary O'Connor, Olivia Petrella, Shawn Pollard, Marne Rubinstein, Samara Shutkind, David Tobin, Samantha Walker, Jennifer Whitman, Vanessa Wipfler, and Nicholas Yarmac.

AND THE INVALUABLE TEAM MEMBERS WHO HAVE COME BEFORE: Andrew Acevedo, Melanie Barton, Elizabeth Beck, Jocelyn Beliveau, Bryan Belmore, Parnel Bogard, Kelly Burke, Gillian Cable-Murphy, Meghan Camirand, Francesca Campo, Jennifer Chan, Bridget Charville, Lauren Cline, Miriam Curran, Erin Davies, Brian Deichmann, Michael Devine, Mark DiSerio, Donna Duquette, Sara Ford, Julie Freed, Rob Froehlich, Alissa Galford, Sara Gottman, Elizabeth Greene, Rebecca Griffing, Allison Grizzell, Beth Grossman, Kenneth Hamilton II, James Hansen, Jennifer Hawkins, Jennifer Hearon, Maureen Hughes, Leslie Jensen, Alexandra Kadar, David Kessler, Amy Kimball, Mariel Koed, Courtney Komlo, Korrine Kotovos, David Krohn, Justyna Kuklinski, Emily Lalone, Faith Larsen, Jessica Leonard, Jennifer Logan, Stacy Lopes, Erika McAuliffe, Siobahn McKenna, Bob Mitza, Kyla Moore, Jessica Morin, Alison Mulholland, Emily Murphy, Michael Navisky, Joshua Oldrid, Marcelo Oliveira, Melanie Owens, Tarryn Prosper, Brian Radlinski, Brittany Rector, Lance Reenstierna, Martine Remy, Abigail Rordorf, Melissa Rousseau, Craig Rubinstein, Kim Rzemien, Jonathan Santarelli, Jennifer Sequeira, Cassandra Shaine, Courtney Smith, Meghan Stock, Kelly Stockley, Kim Stone, Whitney Storrs, Sandi Tarpey Strauss, Tyler Stubbs, Yaxin Tan, Danielle Tauber, Claire Townsend, Morgan Tupper, Nicholas Vargas, Sarah Westervelt, Abigail Wooldridge, Megan Woonton, and Courtney Zentner.

MY EXTRAORDINARY FAMILY: You have always stood by me and encouraged me to make this all happen. Anthony and Carol Ann Rafanelli, Kerry Rafanelli, Carol and Barry Rafanelli, Toni Rafanelli and Joe Kittredge, Beth Rafanelli, Denise Walsh, John Dolan Barry, Shaune and J. Barry, Megan Barry, Kate Barry and Jack Barry, Helen McMahon, Sister Mary Francis Ryan, Jovena and Raymond Lanni, Grace Pera, and Gloria and Pasco Grieco.

AND THE ONE: To Mark Walsh, the person who always keeps me honest and lifts me up (and pulls me down when needed). Thank you, Mr. Walsh.

255

First published in the United States of America in 2019 by
Rizzoli International Publications, Inc.
300 Park Avenue South
New York, NY 10010
www.rizzoliusa.com

Foreword: Chelsea Clinton

Photography Credits:

Roey Yohai: front cover, pages 15, 17-31, back endpapers

Michael Blanchard: front endpapers, reverse of front endpapers, pages 2-4, 135-147, 149-155, 177-181, 183-189, 193-201, 210-215, 220 top left, 222-231, 233-237, 240, 242-243, 245-250, 252, back cover: top row center and right, middle row left and center, bottom row left and center

Matt Teuten: pages 5, 71-79, 157-163, 165, 167-171, 174-175, back cover: middle row right, bottom row right

Allan Zepeda: pages 6, 33-44, 46-49, 51-69, 89-99, 113-125, 238, 255, reverse of back endpapers

Genevieve de Manio Photography: pages 9, 202-207, back cover: top row left

Ayşe Kaya Photography: pages 45, 50

Christian Oth Studio: pages 81-87

Donna Newman: pages 101-111, 241

Carlos Andres Varela: pages 126, 128-133

Nicolaus Czarnecki Photography: pages 177 photos of children, 179-181 photos of children

Matt West Photography: pages 172-173

Getty/Bloomberg: page 191

Ralph Alswang: pages 208-209

Jennifer Domenick / Love Life Images: pages 216-219, 220 top right and bottom three, 221

Brian Phillips: page 244

Lauren Killian: page 251

Cheryl Gerber Photo: page 253

Adrian Nina: author photo

Publisher: Charles Miers
Senior Editor: Kathleen Jayes
Design: Doug Turshen with Steve Turner
Production Manager: Kaija Markoe
Managing Editor: Lynn Scrabis

Printed in China

2019 2020 2021 2022 / 10 9 8 7 6 5 4 3 2 1

ISBN: 978-0-8478-6127-9

Library of Congress Control Number: 2019940040

Visit us online:
Facebook.com/RizzoliNewYork
Twitter: @Rizzoli_Books
Instagram.com/RizzoliBooks
Pinterest.com/RizzoliBooks
Youtube.com/user/RizzoliNY
Issuu.com/Rizzoli